SUCCEED IN

Personnel Management

STUDENT BOOK

N6

Johan van Staden   Melanie Graham

OXFORD
UNIVERSITY PRESS
SOUTH AFRICA

Oxford University Press is a department of the University of Oxford.
It furthers the University's objective of excellence in research, scholarship,
and education by publishing worldwide. Oxford is a registered trade mark of
Oxford University Press in the UK and in certain other countries.

Published in South Africa by
Oxford University Press Southern Africa (Pty) Limited

Vasco Boulevard, Goodwood, N1 City, Cape Town, South Africa, 7460
P O Box 12119, N1 City, Cape Town, South Africa, 7463

Oxford Succeed in Personnel Management N6 Student's Book

ISBN 978 0 19074 741 1

First impression 2019

Acknowledgements
Publisher: Yolandi Farham
Project Manager: Alco Meyer
Designer: Janine Damon
Cover designer: Gisela Strydom
Typesetter: Thomson Digital
Proofreader: Language Mechanics
Indexer: Betsie Greyling
Printed and bound by: Shumani Mills Communications, Parow, Cape Town
SW70390

The authors and publisher gratefully acknowledge permission to reproduce copyright
material in this book. Every effort has been made to trace copyright holders, but if any copyright
infringements have been made, the publisher would be grateful for information that would enable any
omissions or errors to be corrected in subsequent impressions.

Links to third party websites are provided by Oxford in good faith and for information only.
Oxford disclaims any responsibility for the materials contained in any third-party website
referenced in this work.

CONTENTS

MODULE 4

LEADERSHIP

MODULE 5

INFORMATION SYSTEMS AND GRAPHIC REPRESENTATIONS FOR MANAGING HUMAN RESOURCES

HOW TO USE THIS BOOK

Welcome to the Oxford Succeed series for TVET Colleges. *Oxford Succeed in Personnel Management N6* is developed especially for students at this level and provides you with everything you need to excel.

This page will help you understand how the book works.

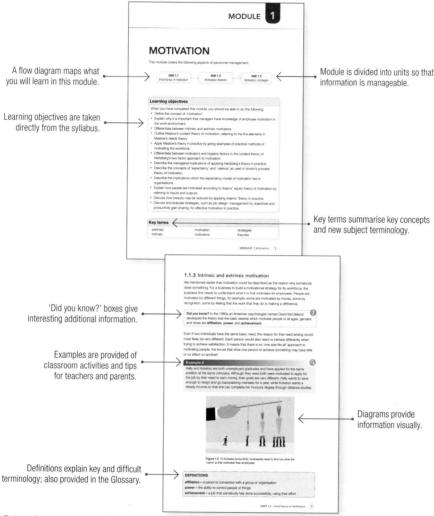

A flow diagram maps what you will learn in this module.

Module is divided into units so that information is manageable.

Learning objectives are taken directly from the syllabus.

Key terms summarise key concepts and new subject terminology.

'Did you know?' boxes give interesting additional information.

Examples are provided of classroom activities and tips for teachers and parents.

Diagrams provide information visually.

Definitions explain key and difficult terminology; also provided in the Glossary.

Other features:
- Headings direct you and tie in explicitly with the syllabus.
- Starting point introduces you to the module.
- Illustrations and photos provide information visually.
- Relevant case studies and real-world articles bring information to life.
- Power Break activities allow for discussion and revision.
- At the end of every module, concise responses to the learning objectives are provided as a summary to use when studying.
- An Assessment section at the end of each module provides test and exam practice.

MOTIVATION

This module covers the following aspects of personnel management:

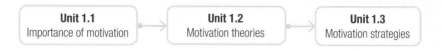

Unit 1.1	Unit 1.2	Unit 1.3
Importance of motivation	Motivation theories	Motivation strategies

Learning objectives

When you have completed this module, you should be able to do the following:
* Define the concept of 'motivation'.
* Explain why it is important that managers have knowledge of employee motivation in the work environment.
* Differentiate between intrinsic and extrinsic motivators.
* Outline Maslow's content theory of motivation, referring to the five elements in Maslow's needs theory.
* Apply Maslow's theory in practice by giving examples of practical methods of motivating the workforce.
* Differentiate between motivators and hygiene factors in the content theory of Hertzberg's two-factor approach to motivation.
* Describe the managerial implications of applying Hertzberg's theory in practice.
* Describe the concepts of 'expectancy' and 'valence' as used in Vroom's process theory of motivation.
* Describe the implications which the expectancy model of motivation has in organisations.
* Explain how people are motivated according to Adams' equity theory of motivation by referring to inputs and outputs.
* Discuss how inequity may be reduced by applying Adams' theory in practice.
* Discuss and evaluate strategies, such as job design, management by objectives and productivity gain-sharing, for effective motivation in practice.

Key terms

extrinsic	motivation	strategies
intrinsic	motivators	theories

Starting point

Verushka has been working at a company for three years. She was extremely excited when she started because the company offered her a competive salary and a great opportunity to develop her skills. In the last three years, she has learnt a great deal and has been involved in some really big projects.

It seems like a perfect job, but Verushka is starting to feel a little bored, and she is not as motivated as before. She thinks that there are not enough challenges for her at work, and no more exciting projects on the horizon. She is unsure of what to do next. She likes the company that she works for, but thinks that if things do not change she might need to look for another job.

In her performance review, Verushka discusses her dilemma with her manager. She explains that she is feeling less motivated than before and is not sure what her next steps should be. Through this conversation, Verushka and her manager work out a growth and development plan for Verushka. In this plan they decide on specific training that Veruska can do to help her do better and be able to move up to the next level within the company.

After this conversation and with this new plan Verushka feels a lot more motivated at work and can clearly see her career path at her current company for at least the next few years.

Figure 1.1 Verushka is motivated to develop her skills within her current company.

UNIT 1.1 Importance of motivation

Employees are increasingly recognised as a business's most valuable **asset** and are more and more being referred to as human capital, rather than personnel or human **resources**. Just like any of the other organisational resources, employees need to be managed so that they work efficiently and effectively to contribute towards achieving the desired objectives and goals of the business. As a personnel manager, you will need to recognise what drives people and understand how they can be encouraged to perform at their best.

1.1.1 What is motivation?

Motivation can be described as the **desire** to be productive, to engage and perform eagerly in one's tasks. A motivated person will feel more invested in their work, and they will strive to be successful.

Motivation is **intentional**, as you need to choose to keep putting in the effort that is required to satisfy your needs or wants. It is also directional because your continued motivation will progressively take you closer to achieving a particular goal. Once you have reached that goal or met a specific need, you will then redirect your efforts into satisfying new needs that arise. Since people have many different needs and wants, this process takes place continuously.

The process of motivation involves three essential elements:
- Motives – things that drive people to act in a certain way
- Behaviour – a series of activities that people do to achieve something
- Goals – the end results that satisfy the motives.

| Motive (needs or wants) | Behaviour (actions) | Goals (end results) |

Figure 1.2 The process of motivation

Example 1.1

If you are feeling hungry, then you will make an effort to go to the kitchen and prepare yourself a meal. Your hunger is a biological need that drives you to perform the action or activities of preparing food. Once you have eaten the meal, your hunger is satisfied, and you no longer have a motive or reason to prepare more food.

DEFINITIONS

asset – a person or thing that is valuable or useful

resources – a supply of something that is available for use, such as money

desire – a strong wish to have or do something

intentional – done deliberately

Having needs or wants that are not being met causes a state of **imbalance** in our lives. People will continuously work to correct this imbalance and achieve satisfaction, but not everyone is willing to put in the same amount of effort. This means that our level of motivation is closely tied to the importance of our goals and our **attitude** towards achieving them. For example, if you really wanted to score higher marks on a test, then you would be more driven to put in the extra hours of study time.

Did you know? The term 'motivate' comes from the Latin word for 'move'. Motivation is said to be the force or energy that keeps moving us towards achieving our goals or satisfying our needs, even when there are obstacles and things do not go our way.

Flashback to N5: In Module 4 of *Succeed in Personnel Management N5* you learned about the importance of having job satisfaction and how this affects employee motivation and productivity.

Figure 1.3 The concept of motivation

Power Break 1.1 INDIVIDUAL WORK

Use what you have learned so far to define the concept of 'motivation' logically in your own words.

DEFINITIONS

imbalance – a situation in which things are not in balance, which causes problems

attitude – the way that you think or feel about something

1.1.2 The importance of employee motivation in the workplace

The work performance of individual employees is usually monitored by managers that are found at the various levels (top, middle and lower) in the organisational structure. For example, a Sales Manager may be appointed to supervise the performance of a company's Sales Representatives. It is up to these managers to coordinate the work efforts of the employees they have authority over. This, in turn, helps the business to function as a whole and to achieve its organisational goals.

Most businesses are started with the broad aims or objectives of achieving profits and growth. **Productivity** is one of the factors that play a significant role in attaining these objectives. A more productive business can manufacture or sell a higher volume of products or provide services to a higher number of customers. Productivity levels increase when your employees can work more **efficiently** and perform their tasks more willingly.

For many years it was assumed that money, higher salaries, and bonuses, would be enough to encourage staff to perform well. Managers focused on improved training opportunities in the belief that good performance came from the employees' ability to get the job done. It is now widely accepted that outstanding employee performance comes from staff both being able to do the job well and wanting to do the job well.

Figure 1.4 Motivated employees work together to achieve business goals.

> **DEFINITIONS**
>
> **productivity** – the rate at which a worker, a company or a country produces goods
> **efficiently** – doing something well with no waste of time or money

It is important that managers understand how the motivation of employees will affect the functioning of the work environment. Some of the benefits of a motivated workforce include:

- Engaged, productive staff can help the business to achieve its goals.
- Staff comes to work more regularly, therefore decreasing absenteeism.
- Employees tend to take more pride in their work and are willing to do extra tasks.
- People remain committed to the business, and the rate of staff turnover is reduced.
- Employees are more willing to learn and are more proactive.
- Satisfied employees are less likely to engage in industrial action.
- Building trust and respect allows for stronger teams to be formed.
- Employees require less supervision and are less likely to make costly mistakes.
- Competitive advantages can be created through excellent customer service.

Managers who show little interest in motivating their staff may find themselves facing resistance when they need to get things done. If employees feel that their needs or wants are not being considered, their motivation levels may begin to decrease. Employees who are not motivated may not perform well in their jobs and can negatively affect the overall success of the business. Some of the risks of having a **demotivated** workforce include:

- A lack of productivity, with increased mistakes or wastage due to carelessness.
- Staff shortages, as employees take more leave or resign from their positions.
- A loss of professionalism or **ethics**, leading to increased incidents of theft, fraud or corruption (such as taking bribes).
- Lost sales, as unhappy staff provide decreasing levels of customer service.
- Employees are more likely to engage in hostile behaviour, such as protests.
- **Disgruntled** employees may damage the organisation's image or reputation.

You will learn more about how managers can use motivation in practice later in this module.

Power Break 1.2   INDIVIDUAL WORK

1   What do you think motivates employees in the workplace? Why do you say so?
2   What are some of the risks of showing little interest in motivating staff?

DEFINITIONS

demotivated – when somebody feels that it is not worth making an effort

ethics – moral principles that control or influence a person's behaviour

disgruntled – annoyed or disappointed

1.1.3 Intrinsic and extrinsic motivation

We mentioned earlier that motivation could be described as the reason why somebody does something. For a business to build a motivational strategy for its workforce, the business first needs to understand what it is that motivates its employees. People are motivated by different things, for example, some are motivated by money, some by recognition, and some by feeling that the work they do is making a difference.

> **Did you know?** In the 1960s an American psychologist named David McClelland developed the theory that the basic desires which motivate people of all ages, genders and races are **affiliation**, **power** and **achievement**.

Even if two individuals have the same basic need, the reason for that need arising would most likely be very different. Each person would also react or behave differently when trying to achieve satisfaction. It means that there is no 'one size fits all' approach to motivating people; the forces that drive one person to achieve something may have little or no effect on another!

Example 1.2

Kelly and Koketso are both unemployed graduates and have applied for the same position at the same company. Although they were both motivated to apply for the job by their need to earn money, their goals are very different. Kelly wants to save enough to resign and go backpacking overseas for a year, while Koketso wants a steady income so that she can complete her Honours degree through distance studies.

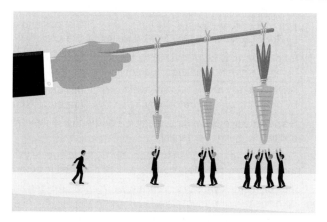

Figure 1.5 To increase productivity, businesses need to find out what the 'carrot' is that motivates their employees.

DEFINITIONS

affiliation – a person's connection with a group or organisation

power – the ability to control people or things

achievement – a job that somebody has done successfully, using their effort

Motivators can be grouped into intrinsic (internal) and extrinsic (external) factors. *Intrinsic motivation* comes from within yourself, while *extrinsic motivation* comes from something outside of yourself.

Example 1.3

In Starting point, you saw how Verushka was motivated by both the extrinsic (external) drive to earn a competitive salary, and her intrinsic (internal) desire to develop her skills.

Let's take a closer look at the differences between intrinsic and extrinsic motivation.

In the work environment, intrinsic motivation refers to the satisfaction or sense of fulfilment that a person gets from the job itself. For example, a student who finds the subject that they are studying fascinating may strive to read more widely, and gains satisfaction from understanding more about the topic. It is the student's feelings about the subject that provide the intrinsic (internal) motivation for them to read more about it. Table 1.1 provides some examples of intrinsic motivators for employees in the workplace.

Table 1.1 Intrinsic motivators

Method	Explanation
Being recognised	Feeling that they are accepted and treated as a valuable individual can give employees an increased sense of pride and self-worth.
Task variety	Working on a range of different tasks can prevent boredom and provide the **mental stimulus** that certain employees look for in a job.
Being challenged	Some people are always looking for new challenges and are motivated by doing work which they find interesting and exciting.
Taking responsibility	Employees may be motivated by taking on added responsibility and being given opportunities to demonstrate their leadership skills.
Having choices	Being able to choose how the work gets done can motivate employees by providing greater **autonomy**.
Developing skills	Some employees are motivated by a desire to use their talents, skills and abilities to their full potential.
Setting the pace	Employees who are given the opportunity to determine the speed at which they work may feel more confident in their abilities to cope with demands.
Participative decision-making	Including employees in organisational decision-making and valuing their opinions can give them a feeling of belonging and accomplishment.
Career opportunities	Employees may be motivated by the feeling that they can grow with the company and help in shaping its future.

DEFINITIONS

mental stimulus – something that is more interesting and challenging to your mind
autonomy – the ability to act and make decisions without being controlled
participative – allowing everyone to give opinions and to help make decisions

Power Break 1.3 INDIVIDUAL WORK

1 Why did you decide to further your studies? List the factors that motivated you.
2 If you were an employee, what do you think would drive you to work harder?
3 Analyse each of the elements you identified in the previous questions. Would you say that any of these factors are examples of intrinsic motivation? Give a reason for your answer.

Did you know? Intrinsic motivation is an essential factor to consider when designing training courses, as employees are more likely to participate if they find the activities interesting and exciting!

Extrinsic motivation in the work environment refers to the offers of rewards or threats of punishment that are affected through company policies and practices. For example, **incentive** schemes can offer rewards such as free holidays or cash bonuses for employees who meet performance targets. However, some employees may also be motivated to reach the goals by the fear of losing their jobs if they don't perform well. These external forces usually originate from managers in an attempt to bring employee behaviour in line with the organisation's expectations and goals.

The extrinsic motivators can be further classified into financial (monetary) rewards or non-financial rewards. For example, even though a student may find a particular subject boring, he or she could still strive to get good marks because it will lead to a high-paying career (financial reward) with a secure job (non-financial compensation). In this example, the student was motivated to study by outside influences, rather than their feelings or opinions about the subject. Table 1.2 provides some examples of extrinsic motivators for employees in the workplace.

Table 1.2 Examples of extrinsic motivators

Method	Explanation
Monetary rewards	Earning a fair salary, financial bonuses, annual increases, shares, fringe benefits (company car, fuel allowance, medical aid, pension, etc.)
Promotion opportunities	Opportunities to move into higher positions with more impressive job titles, which usually require taking on added responsibilities.
Recognition	Being considered an expert source of advice or earning praise and recognition for an outstanding contribution to the success of the company.
Job security	Contract workers or temporary employees may be motivated by the opportunity to impress their superiors and secure a permanent position.
Working conditions	Employees may be motivated by the offer of a bigger office with a more beautiful view, better staff meals or the promise of safer working conditions.
Good leadership	Leaders who are competent set a good example and treat employees justly may inspire their staff to perform at their best.
Realistic expectations	Managers can motivate employees to meet expectations by providing clear instructions and setting reasonable targets that are achievable.

DEFINITION

incentive – something that encourages you to do something

Power Break 1.4   INDIVIDUAL WORK

Read the following scenario carefully and then answer the questions that follow.

Aggie has worked on contract as computer practice lecturer at a TVET college for the past six years. She enjoys interacting with her students and recently received a staff award for achieving excellent pass rates. Aggie feels a great sense of achievement when she watches her students graduate, especially since the conditions on campus are not always ideal. Some of the computers in Aggie's classroom are broken, and she often has to buy her paper to make photocopies. Aggie has applied for a permanent position as a senior lecturer, as she would like to use her experience to mentor the newer staff members.

1   Can you identify Aggie's extrinsic motivators?
2   Can you identify Aggie's intrinsic motivators?
3   Can you identify any factors that could cause Aggie to become demotivated?
4   What else could Aggie's campus manager do to improve her motivation?

UNIT 1.2 **Motivation theories**

Since being able to control and direct the efforts of employees is a critical factor in the successful management of an organisation, extensive research has been undertaken to figure out how best to achieve this. Psychologists and other behavioural experts have developed many theories that attempt to explain how or why motivation happens.

A theory is a set of ideas that try to provide reasons why something happens the way that it does. Theories are often used to explain the cause-and-effect relationships between a group of factors.

The motivational theories that you are going to learn about can be grouped into two categories: content theories and process theories. Content theories focus on what motivates people's behaviour, while process theories are concerned with how motivation takes place.

Figure 1.6 Some popular theories of motivation

Maslow's hierarchy of needs

Probably the best-known theory of motivation is Abraham Maslow's **hierarchy** of needs. Maslow formulated a motivation theory that explains human needs according to a needs hierarchy. He classified human needs into five main hierarchical groups, as illustrated in figure 1.7.

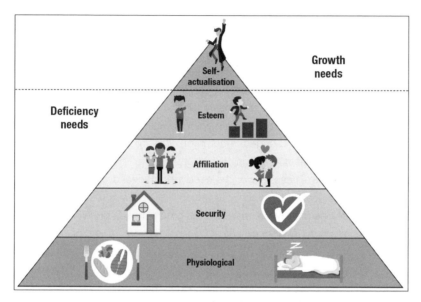

Figure 1.7 Maslow's hierarchy of needs

Maslow classified the fundamental or basic human needs as lower-order needs. These include physiological needs, safety and security needs and social needs. He believed that people need to satisfy these fundamental needs first, before the higher-order needs for esteem, status and self-fulfilment would develop.

Example 1.4

In Starting point, you saw how Verushka struggled to stay motivated even though the company offered her a competitive salary which would satisfy her lower-order needs.

The five levels in Maslow's hierarchy include the following:

- **Physiological needs**: These are the most basic needs that have to be satisfied for a person to survive. Examples include the need for shelter, clothing, food, oxygen, water, bodily functioning, and sleep. If these needs are not being satisfied, a person will direct

---

DEFINITION

hierarchy – a system that ideas or beliefs can be arranged into

their behaviour at satisfying them. Once these needs are met, the next level of needs begins to motivate an individual.

- **Safety and security needs**: This level refers to the need for protection against physical harm, such as accidents and war. It also includes the need for economic security from poverty and the familiar, rather than the unknown or unexpected.
- **Social needs**: Only when our physiological and safety and security needs are satisfied can we meet our social needs: the need for love, affection and companionship. These needs can also be referred to as affiliation needs, as humans feel the need to belong to a particular group.
- **Esteem and status needs**: These needs involve what people think of themselves (their self-concept) and what others think of them (status and respect). They include the need for power, achievement, independence and self-confidence. The needs for status and belonging to a group are closely related. Not only do we have an obligation to be accepted by our peers, but we also want to excel beyond others' achievements and have our results acknowledged. A common complaint of employees on this level is that management does not recognise their attempts to shine.
- **Self-fulfilment needs**: These refer to the need for personal development and the use of all our talents, abilities and potential: to become all that we are capable of becoming. These needs are also referred to as growth needs or self-actualisation needs. Getting a sought-after qualification or writing a book, poem or song will satisfy these needs.

> **Did you know?** There has been much debate around the classification of Maslow's hierarchy of needs into lower order or higher order needs. It is important to remember that people from different cultures, regions or age groups may **rank** their needs in a different order.

Power Break 1.5 GROUP WORK

Working in your groups, read the following statement and then answer the questions that follow.

The National Minimum Wage Bill was passed by parliament on 30 May 2018. It is estimated that over 6 million South Africans will benefit from an increase in income.

1 Which needs of employees are most likely to be satisfied with the introduction of this bill?
2 Will the introduction of a minimum wage lead to improved productivity in South Africa?
3 What are the negative implications of passing this bill? How could these affect the employee's motivation?

DEFINITION

rank – to give something a particular position on a scale according to its importance

The implications of Maslow's theory of motivation for the workplace include:

- Needs that are already being satisfied no longer provide motivation. For example, employees who already earn a higher-than-average income may not be motivated by additional monetary incentives.
- Employees all have different combinations of needs. For example, something that is a motivator for one employee may not work for another.
- Managers will need to understand the specific combinations of needs of each individual in their team.
- People can move up or down the hierarchy, depending on their current situation. For example, an employee's needs may change over time due to their circumstances.

Examples of practical methods of motivating the workforce

Table 1.3 provides practical methods of how managers can apply Maslow's needs theory in practice.

Table 1.3 Examples of Maslow's needs in the workplace

Need	Examples
Physiological needs	Lunch breaks, staff meals, exercise and recreational facilities, rest periods, holidays, sick leave, etc.
Safety and security needs	A basic salary, medical aid, pension schemes, unemployment insurance, job security, safe working environment, etc.
Social needs	Friendship with colleagues, team-building activities, participation, and involvement in departmental and organisational activities, etc.
Esteem and status needs	Recognition, promotion opportunities, award ceremonies, incentive schemes, etc.
Self-fulfilment needs	Further education, in-service training, increased autonomy, exciting projects, opportunities for charity or community work, etc.

Power Break 1.6 INDIVIDUAL WORK

Read the following scenario carefully and then answer the questions that follow.

Jabu recently completed matric and was unemployed for four months before he was offered the opportunity to train as a waiter in a nearby restaurant. After struggling to get enough to eat for so long, he was very grateful that the trainees received a meal at the end of each training session. Now that his stomach was full, Jabu could concentrate better on the training materials, and he passed his waiters test with flying colours! The restaurant owner was very impressed and immediately offered Jabu a permanent position. The other staff made Jabu feel very welcome and encouraged him to join the company soccer team. Jabu loved being at the restaurant and worked very hard to keep his customers happy. Within a year he had already won the employee of the month award twice! The owner was so pleased with his dedication that he decided to give Jabu a bursary to study hospitality management at the local college.

1 Identify appropriate examples from the scenario that match each of the five elements of Maslow's needs theory.

continued on the next page …

2 If Jabu were to lose his job through retrenchment, do you think that he would remain focused on his self-fulfilment needs? Explain your answer.
3 Do you think that the invitation to join the company soccer team would be a motivator for all the other waiters too? Give reasons for your answer.

Herzberg's two-factor theory

Frederick Herzberg developed and proposed the dual-factor theory of motivation, which is also known as the motivation-hygiene theory. In his research, he asked people to describe situations in which they felt excellent, or bad, about their jobs. So, he investigated the central question: What do people want from their jobs?

Herzberg's theory is based on the view that people have two primary needs:
- The need for psychological growth and achievement (motivation factors)
- The need to avoid harm from the environment (hygiene factors).

Motivators and hygiene factors

Motivation factors are inherent to the contents of the job itself and are called intrinsic factors. These include aspects such as achievement and recognition, which are related to job satisfaction.

The hygiene factors, on the other hand, occur in the work environment and are outside the scope of the job itself. So, they are called extrinsic factors. Hygiene factors include the necessities of any job, such as a salary. These factors must be present to prevent employee dissatisfaction. They are a precondition for positive, true motivation to take place. However, the presence of hygiene factors on their own will not motivate employees.

Figure 1.8 provides some examples of motivation factors and hygiene factors.

Motivation factors (satisfiers)
- the work itself
- achievement
- recognition and praise (feedback)
- responsibility
- advancement (promotion)
- personal growth

Hygiene factors (dissatisfiers)
- salary
- service conditions
- equipment
- job security
- fringe benefits
- interpersonal relationships
- status
- supervision
- administration and policies

Figure 1.8 Motivators and hygiene factors in Herzberg's dual-factor theory

Did you know? Herzberg's hygiene factors correspond to Maslow's physiological, safety and security needs. His motivation factors correspond to Maslow's needs for status, respect and self-fulfilment.

Managerial implications of Herzberg's theory of motivation for the workplace

Managerial implications of Herzberg's theory of motivation for the workplace include:

* Employees that are dissatisfied cannot be motivated.
* Managers need first to ensure that the hygiene factors are present to avoid staff becoming dissatisfied, before introducing the motivators.
* Employees are driven by work that allows them to make real achievements.
* The achievements of employees need to be recognised.
* The job itself needs to be designed in a manner that is interesting and challenging.

You will learn more about how job design can be used as a motivation strategy later in this module.

Power Break 1.7 INDIVIDUAL WORK

Use a table to show the relation between the two motivation theories (Maslow and Herzberg).

Vroom's expectancy theory

Expectancy and valence

One of the most valid and widely accepted explanations of motivation is Victor Vroom's **expectancy** theory (Robbins 2003).

Victor Vroom's expectancy theory is widely accepted as a simplified explanation of motivation. According to his theory, people are more motivated if they believe that their behaviour will result in an outcome that is appealing to them. In other words, people's motivation to exert effort (to do something) depends on their expectations for success.

Vroom's process theory of motivation is based on three key concepts, as illustrated in figure 1.9.

> **DEFINITION**
>
> **expectancy** – the state of expecting or hoping that something will happen

These concepts can also be described as relationships:

- **The effort-performance relationship (expectancy)**: An individual's expectation that exerting a certain level of effort will lead to visible performance.
- **The performance-reward relationship (instrumentality)**: The degree to which an individual believes that performing at a particular level will lead to the achievement of the desired outcome (reward).
- **The rewards-personal goals relationship (valence)**: The degree to which organisational rewards satisfy an individual's personal goals or needs and the attractiveness of those potential rewards for the individual (Robbins 2003).

Figure 1.9 Key concepts of Vroom's theory of motivation

In practical terms, Vroom's expectancy theory says that if a student believes that by working harder she will achieve higher marks (expectancy), and that higher marks will lead to securing a place at university and a sought-after career (instrumentality), and that these rewards will satisfy her personal goals (valence), then these expectations should lead to a higher level of motivation within her.

Implications of Vroom's theory of motivation for the workplace

The impact of Vroom's theory of motivation for the workplace include:

- Employees will be motivated to perform better if they believe that their efforts will lead to achievements that will satisfy their personal goals.
- Managers need to realise that employees may place different values on the same reward. For example, some people may value the status of a job title (such as CEO) very highly, while for others their job title may be of much less importance.
- Different employees may view the relationships between effort, performance and reward in different ways. For example, managers will need to be very clear when communicating the performance criteria and how these criteria relate to rewards.
- Employees need to view performance standards as achievable. For example, managers may need to consult with employees to set reasonable and attainable targets that will be effective motivators.
- Employees need adequate support, information and resources (such as equipment) to improve their performance.

> **DEFINITION**
>
> **valence** – the value individuals place on results based on their needs, goals, values, and sources of motivation

Figure 1.10 Employees are more productive when they believe that their expectations will be realised.

Power Break 1.8   INDIVIDUAL WORK

Read the following scenario carefully and then answer the questions that follow.

John and Peter are both employed as petrol attendants at a local service station. The Personnel Manager recently informed them that the position of forecourt supervisor would become vacant soon, as the current supervisor is due to retire in a few months' time. John immediately began to take extra care when serving customers, as he believes that their positive feedback will convince the supervisor to recommend him for the position. John has always wanted to own a car and getting the promotion would finally make his dream possible! Peter, on the other hand, feels that no amount of hard work will lead to a promotion. He has heard a rumour that management posts are always advertised externally, so he doesn't see the point of making any extra effort for a goal that he feels is unattainable.

1 Describe the concepts of expectancy, instrumentality and valence as used in Vroom's process theory of motivation with the aid of practical examples from this scenario.
2 What practical steps could the forecourt supervisor take to influence Peter's motivation?

Adams' theory of fairness

Equity theory of motivation

Behavioural psychologist John Stacey Adams developed the **equity** theory of motivation, which is also known as the theory of fairness. He proposed that people attach great importance to fairness and will be motivated when they feel that they are being rewarded equally. On the other hand, if people think that they are being treated unfairly, they are more likely to become demotivated. Although this idea seems relatively straightforward, his theory of how employees determine fairness is far more complex.

Adams' equity theory is based on the following concepts:

- What employees put into the job (inputs or costs)
- What benefits employees get out of the job (outputs or rewards)
- How employees perceive their **ratio** of inputs and outputs to compare to the ratio of inputs and outputs of others (comparison process).

Inputs include everything that an employee contributes to his or her work. Inputs can include hard work, commitment, dedication, enthusiasm, etc. Employees view these contributions as what **entitles** them to earn rewards. Outputs are the outcomes which employees see as the consequences of their efforts and their relationship with the employer (organisation). Outputs include tangible benefits, such as pay, and intangible rewards, like being thanked. Figure 1.11 provides some additional examples of inputs and outputs.

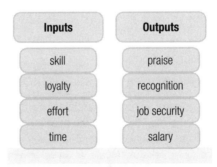

Inputs	Outputs
skill	praise
loyalty	recognition
effort	job security
time	salary

Figure 1.11 Balancing inputs and outputs in Adams' equity theory

---

DEFINITIONS

equity – a situation in which everyone is treated equally

ratio – the relationship between two groups of people or things

entitles – gives somebody the right to have or do something

People tend to be satisfied with their jobs when the ratio of inputs to outputs is very close. If a person feels that they put in much more than they get out, they may reduce their efforts, become angry or disruptive, or leave the organisation. However, merely balancing inputs and outputs is not enough to ensure employee motivation.

Equity also depends on an employee's comparison of their ratio of inputs and outputs to those of their relational partners in the work environment. Relational partners are other people who are seen to be in a similar situation, such as co-workers or colleagues. Employees may also make comparisons with people who perform a similar role in other organisations or even evaluate their present situation against working for their previous employer.

Example 1.5

Thuli and Thandi both earn the same salary as receptionists at a medical centre. Thuli works from 7 am until 4 pm from Mondays to Fridays. She enjoys her job and has always felt that the organisation compensates her well for her efforts. However, Thuli recently heard the office manager telling Thandi that she may leave work at 3 pm from now on because she needs to collect her child from preschool. Thuli feels that this is very unfair. Thandi had agreed to work half-days on Saturdays to make up for leaving earlier during the week, but Thuli was not aware of this arrangement.

In Example 1.5 you saw how Thuli was satisfied with her job when she thought that her inputs (time) to outputs (salary) ratio was the same as Thandi's. This example is further illustrated in Figure 1.12 below. When Thuli realised that Thandi would be receiving the same salary for working fewer hours, she began to experience a feeling of unfairness or inequity. Even though Thuli's own working conditions have not changed, her level of motivation and her working relationships with Thandi and the office manager could be negatively affected by the perception that her colleague was enjoying a better reward-to-effort ratio.

Figure 1.12 In Adams' theory of fairness, employees feel satisfied when their input/output ratio is perceived as being equal to that of their co-workers.

The implications of Adams' theory of motivation for the workplace include the following:
- Individuals will strive to get the most outputs (rewards) for their inputs (efforts).
- When people work in a team or group, such as in an organisation, they will continuously compare their efforts and rewards to those of others.
- If any perceived or actual inequities arise, employees will become dissatisfied.
- Changing the pay or working conditions of one employee can demotivate others.
- Employees may accept a certain amount of inequity if they feel that the other person is entitled to more benefits, for example, through their position in the organisation.

- The values that each employee assigns to their inputs and outputs will be different, even if they perform the same work for the same pay.
- Employees are capable of adjusting to the conditions in which an organisation operates. For example, accepting lower salaries in small towns where the cost of living is cheaper.

How to reduce inequity

A difference in pay is a common reason why employees feel unfairly treated, but inequities can also arise from bad decision-making by management, a lack of feedback or recognition, and limited opportunities for career development. Whether the **allegations** of unfairness are real or not, they will still increase dissatisfaction, and may have a negative effect on employee **morale**, motivation and productivity. For this reason, both the organisation and employees will do their best to eliminate the distress and restore equity in the workplace. Figure 1.13 shows some of the ways in which employees and managers may try to reduce the suffering caused by inequity.

Employees' methods to reduce inequity

- They increase their efforts to get a bigger reward.
- They complain to managers and demand changes to rewards.
- They put in less effort or take less care in their work.
- They remove themselves from the situation by resigning.
- They convince themselves that the relational partner is a unique case.
- They compare with another employee whose situation is more similar.

Managers' methods to reduce inequity

- They identify and address underlying problems causing dissatisfaction.
- They treat all employees fairly and avoid **favouritism**.
- They apply company rules, policies and procedures consistently.
- They keep communication channels open and encourage regular feedback.
- They manage employees' perceptions of their own and others' ratios.
- They involve employees in the choice of rewards or outcomes.
- They adjust employees' inputs, e.g. reducing workloads or working hours.
- They give praise and recognition to all manner of efforts and achievements.
- They provide opportunities for career development and promotion.

Figure 1.13 Methods to reduce inequity in practice

DEFINITIONS

allegations – accusing somebody of doing something that is wrong or illegal

morale – the amount of confidence or enthusiasm, etc., that a person or a group has at a particular time

favouritism – the act of unfairly treating one person better than others because you like them better

Power break 1.9   INDIVIDUAL WORK

Go back and read the scenario in Example 1.5 again.

1   Are Thuli's feelings of inequity real or perceived? Give reasons for your answer.
2   What steps do you think Thuli would follow to maintain equity in this situation?
3   What steps should the office manager follow to improve Thuli's motivation?
4   Explain how this situation could also have a negative effect on Thandi's motivation.

UNIT 1.3 **Motivation strategies**

Motivation theories or models help us to understand what motivation is and how it works, but managers also need **strategies** which can be used to **implement** effective motivation in practice. Figure 1.14 illustrates some of the motivation strategies that managers can use in the workplace.

| Job design | Management by objectives | Productivity gain-sharing |

Figure 1.14 Strategies for effective motivation

1.3.1 Job design

Job design is an internal process in which the Human Resources Department decides how work is arranged into responsibilities, duties, and tasks. Job design is also sometimes referred to as task design or work design. Job redesign is considered when the structure of the existing job needs to change and has to be redesigned. Job design and redesign aim to improve efficiency and employee job satisfaction.

To design jobs effectively, you have to:
- first, have a thorough understanding of the job (through job analysis)
- identify all the components of the job (tasks, goals, skills needed)
- take into account job efficiency (best way to carry out the job and meet goals)
- assess the workspace (is it well organised?)
- look at the work environment and equipment (the health and safety of employees are essential).

> **DEFINITIONS**
>
> **strategies** – methods to achieve a particular purpose, or solve a problem
> **implement** – to make something start to happen

Flashback to N4: In Module 4 of *Succeed in Personnel Management N4* you learned how job design begins with the process of job analysis, which results in a job description and a list of job specifications.

Job enlargement or enrichment

The way in which jobs are designed can have a significant impact on the effectiveness of the organisation. Jobs should motivate employees by being exciting and satisfying. People want to engage in meaningful work. Personnel managers have to make sure that the job design balances the needs of the organisation with the needs of the employee. If job design is done correctly, employees will be motivated and efficient, and productivity levels and profits will increase. Table 1.4 outlines some of the techniques which can be used in job design.

Table 1.4 Techniques used in job design

Technique	Explanation	Example
Job enlargement	This happens when additional responsibilities are allocated to an employee on a horizontal level. The job is enlarged by adding additional related tasks. Using this technique can relieve the **monotony** and make the job more challenging and exciting, provided that adequate training is given. The aim is to prevent the employee from becoming bored and demotivated if there are not many opportunities for promotion. Job enlargement can also create more flexibility within the workforce, as employees can perform a greater variety of activities.	Adding a secretarial responsibility to a receptionist's job to make the position more challenging.
Job enrichment	This happens when the level of responsibility is increased, and more challenges are added. The employee is given more authority, freedom and control over the way the job is done. As opposed to job enlargement, job enrichment is a vertical expansion of the job, giving the employee the chance to upgrade their skills or use skills in more challenging ways by taking on tasks that are usually allocated to higher positions. As with job enlargement, the aim is to increase job satisfaction and motivation levels.	Asking a senior sales assistant to fill in for the sales manager (who is on leave) at the weekly management meeting.
Job rotation	Job rotation is a job design technique that gives employees the opportunity to perform different jobs and learn new skills by systematically moving them from one job to the next over a period. Job rotation makes people more versatile and increases employee satisfaction by exposing the employee to different experiences.	Rotating the production foreman into a sales assistant position to give them a better understanding of customer needs.
Job simplification	This technique breaks jobs down into simple tasks which are repeated continuously. The objective is to improve productivity by reducing the amount of physical or mental effort that is required to do the job. Job simplification results in jobs that require few skills or little experience.	Splitting the tasks performed by a secretary into two separate positions: a typist and a receptionist.

> **DEFINITION**
>
> **monotony** – boring, lack of variety

Flashback to N5: The advantages and disadvantages of job enrichment and job rotation were discussed in detail in Module 4 of *Succeed in Personnel Management N5*.

Figure 1.15 Repetitive jobs can benefit from job rotation.

Power Break 1.10 INDIVIDUAL WORK

Read the following scenario carefully and then answer the questions that follow.

Jeshan and Grace both work for a large agricultural company that grows, processes, packs and sells thousands of avocados each year. Jeshan's job is to record the weight of each crate of avocados that arrives from the plantations. Although he enjoys chatting to the tractor drivers, he sometimes gets tired of doing the same task over and over each day. Grace works in the administration office as a creditors clerk. Her job involves checking the invoices for packaging materials and making sure the accounts are paid on time each month.

1 Which job design technique was most likely used in the design of Jeshan's job?
2 Do you think Jeshan is motivated? Give reasons for your answer.
3 Explain how job rotation could improve Jeshan's motivation.
4 Discuss how each of the techniques of job enlargement and job enrichment could be used to redesign Grace's job.

1.3.2 Management by objectives

Management by objectives (MBO) is a management tool which is used to set goals (objectives) and evaluate performance. Managers and employees work together to develop objectives that **align** the goals of the individual employee with those of the organisation. These objectives then become the performance standards against which an employee's efforts can be measured and rewarded.

Key point: Good objectives should be SMART:

- Use SPECIFIC terms to describe your goals (who? what? why? when? how?).
- Include MEASURABLE amounts in figures.
- Ensure that they are ACHIEVABLE with the available budget and resources.
- Keep them REALISTIC for the size and type of organisation.
- Set an end date for TIMELY completion.

Figure 1.16 The characteristics of a well-written objective

A key aspect of management by objectives is determining how goals should be set. A business's vision and mission are the starting point for creating organisational goals. These broad, overall objectives are then translated into more specific departmental objectives for each functional area of the business. Departmental managers work together with each employee to set individual goals that support the achievement of the departmental objectives. This process ensures that employees have a clear understanding of their role in the organisation and of how their actions contribute to its overall success.

Did you know? The principles of management by objectives (MBO), also known as Management by results (MBR), were developed by Peter Drucker in his book *The Practice of Management*.

DEFINITION

align – to be in the correct position to something else

Some of the tasks involved in putting management by objectives into practice include:

* setting SMART objectives which challenge and motivate employees
* encouraging employee participation in developing personal objectives
* monitoring and measuring employees' progress towards achieving objectives
* providing daily feedback to encourage personal growth and development
* evaluating employee performance and rewarding achievements
* deciding on actions that can lead to improvements.

The aim of management by objectives is to improve employee motivation by encouraging employees to participate in the organisation's planning process. Employees are more committed to helping the organisation reach its goals when they have a say in the results that must be achieved and can decide on the most efficient way in which to achieve them.

Many well-known organisations attribute their success to using management by objectives. However, there are also managers who criticise this approach. Table 1.5 discusses some of the advantages and disadvantages of using management by objectives to motivate your workforce.

Table 1.5 The benefits and risks of management by objectives as a motivation strategy

Advantages	Disadvantages
Employees are motivated when they understand the importance of their role and responsibilities in the organisation.	Managers may not have the required training or understanding to implement this process successfully.
Objectives can be used as performance standards to measure employee efforts.	Objectives that are vague or unclear cannot be used to measure performance.
Achieving objectives increases job satisfaction and therefore motivation.	People who have a strong personality may intimidate others when setting goals.
Employees are empowered by being included in the decision-making process.	Decisions take much longer as everybody needs to be involved in the process.
Continual monitoring of employees allows for more effective control.	Employees may attempt to **distort** results to meet short-term targets.
Linking organisational objectives to personal goals encourages commitment.	The quality of the work itself may decrease if employees only focus on achieving results.
Organisational objectives provide direction through a common goal for all departments to work towards.	Tracking and recording employee performance can be time-consuming and involve much extra administrative work.
Reliable management information systems provide valuable feedback.	Targets may remain unachievable if all contributing factors are not identified.
Daily consultation and interaction improve communication.	Employees may become too focused on achieving their objectives.

DEFINITION

distort – to twist or change facts so that they are no longer right or true

Power Break 1.11 INDIVIDUAL WORK

Read the following scenario carefully and then answer the questions that follow.

Joy works in the customer care department of a company specialising in software development and sales. Joy's role is to provide callers with step-by-step instructions on how to install new software on their computers. The customer care manager recently held a meeting to inform employees that the organisation would be implementing the management by objectives system and employees would be rewarded for achieving their respective targets. Working with her departmental manager, Joy set the objective of completing each customer call within 8 minutes. It would reduce caller waiting times and allow Joy to assist more customers each day. At the end of the first month, Joy is disappointed to hear that she will not be receiving a reward since her average call time was over 10 minutes per customer. Joy feels that this is very unfair, as many of her callers struggle with technology and keep asking her to repeat the instructions. She decides to limit all future calls by shortening her greeting and avoiding any small talk.

1 Do you think that Joy and her manager did an excellent job of setting the performance standards? Give a reason for your answer.
2 Do you think that the customer care manager correctly understands the process of management by objectives? Provide evidence to support your answer.
3 Do you think that this experience has affected Joy's motivation? Explain your answer.
4 How will Joy's new strategy to meet her target change her customer service?

1.3.3 Productivity gain-sharing

We mentioned previously that productivity levels increase when your employees can work more efficiently and perform their tasks more willingly. Increased productivity usually leads to the more cost-effective use of resources, as employees use less labour (time) or materials to get the job done. It means that improving productivity is an essential objective of many organisations.

Productivity gain-sharing is an incentive plan that encourages groups of employees, such as teams or departments, to work together to improve their productivity. By working smarter, the group can save the organisation money. These savings are then distributed among the group members using a formula that calculates how much costs have been reduced when compared to a specific target or past results.

> **Flashback to N5**: In Module 3 of *Succeed in Personnel Management N5* you learned about profit sharing as a type of incentive scheme. Productivity gain-sharing is often confused with profit sharing, which is when individual employees are given an incentive based on the profitability of the business.

Figure 1.17 Sharing the gains can reduce conflict between managers and employees.

Productivity gain-sharing requires a participative management style. Managers need to involve employees in decision-making and encourage them to share ideas. Employees have to learn to co-operate with each other and work together as a team to achieve 'gains'. Employee motivation and morale increases when the group realises that they will benefit whenever they help the organisation to save money.

Methods to implement motivation

Now that you have a better understanding of the motivation theories and strategies, you should be able to combine everything that you have learned so far and apply it in practice. Taking into consideration the varied needs of each employee, you can do the following:

- Recognise the importance of both intrinsic and extrinsic motivators.
- Keep employees informed; ensure that there are good communication structures in place and opportunities for feedback.
- Encourage healthy competition and provide recognition for work well done (e.g. rewards such as an employee of the month reward).
- Ensure that there are opportunities for promotion.
- Provide ongoing coaching, training and development opportunities.
- Provide motivational workshops, teambuilding events, and social events to promote staff morale.
- Offer an excellent salary package, with appropriate fringe benefits, such as bonuses or medical aid.
- Ensure safe and healthy working conditions, taking into account hygiene factors (e.g. air conditioners/fans) and social conditions (break room/cafeteria).
- Get to know your employees; learn more about them and treat them as individuals.

- Provide employee support programmes or access to these (e.g. counselling or rehabilitation programmes where needed).
- Promote family welfare if possible (e.g. bursaries for dependents or onsite child-care).
- Ensure that you use a style of management that motivates your workers (e.g. a participative management style that encourages communication, teamwork, and participation in decision-making).

Power Break 1.12   GROUP WORK

Read the article carefully and then answer the questions that follow.

Organisational culture expert Siphiwe Moyo's insights on motivation

Ultimately, it all comes down to whether an individual is in the right job, position, and department. There must be a job and culture fit. In my experience, organisations often don't look closely enough at culture. They look at the right skill sets when hiring, but don't consider the individual.

You can have the same person, with the same skills, in the same position, thriving in one organisation and a disaster in another. If someone isn't performing optimally, start by asking if there's a culture fit or a mismatch.

If there's a mismatch, consider moving the individual to a different department. They might excel in a different role. I've had personal experience with this. As a star performer, I was promoted to a middle management role. On paper, it looked great — a better title, more responsibility, and a salary increase.

Once I started the role, I realised it was the wrong fit for me. I went from being a star performer to mediocre at best. Because I was able to have an open and honest discussion with the organisation, I was able to move into a different role, and ended up being awarded employee of the year again.

As an organisation, keep lines of communication open and allow employees the space to feel safe enough to voice these concerns. People are often too scared to speak up, and so remain stuck in a role they hate and aren't performing in. It's a waste of time and resources for everyone.

Source: Nadine Todd, 18 May 2017. Available at www.entrepreneursmag.co.za

1   Moyo states that 'There must be a job and culture fit'. Do you agree? Work in your groups to discuss this statement.
2   Moyo's promotion into middle management resulted in a decrease in his motivation. Use any suitable theory of motivation to explain why you think this happened.
3   What advice does Moyo give on keeping employees motivated? List three items.

What have we learned about Personnel Management and where to next?

In this module, we learned about motivation. We started by discussing the importance of motivation and why managers need knowledge of employee motivation in the work environment. We went on to discuss the various motivation theories. Lastly, we looked at the strategies that can be used for effective motivation in practice.

In the next module, we will learn about communication.

Revisiting the learning objectives

Now that you have completed this module let's see if you have achieved the learning outcomes that were set out at the beginning of the module. In the table below, we summarise what you have learned for each objective.

Learning objective	What have you learned	✓
Define the concept of 'motivation'.	The concept of motivation includes: • the reason why somebody does something • the drive or desire to satisfy needs or wants • the force that moves people towards attaining goals.	☐
Explain why it is important that managers have knowledge of employee motivation in the work environment.	Managers use employee motivation to: • make employees want to do something • encourage hard work and effort • achieve departmental and organisational goals • improve efficiency and productivity.	☐
Differentiate between intrinsic and extrinsic motivators.	Motivators can be classified as intrinsic or extrinsic: • Intrinsic motivators are the internal feelings within a person, which can cause them to become motivated. • Extrinsic motivators are the external things outside of a person, which can cause them to become motivated.	☐
Outline Maslow's content theory of motivation, referring to the five elements in Maslow's needs theory.	The five elements of Maslow's needs theory are: • physiological needs • safety and security needs • social needs • esteem and status needs • self-fulfilment needs.	☐
Apply Maslow's theory in practice by giving examples of practical methods of motivating the workforce.	Refer to Table 1.3.	☐

Differentiate between motivators and hygiene factors in the content theory of Herzberg's two-factor approach to motivation.	Herzberg's two-factor approach includes: • motivation factors – the need for psychological growth and achievement • hygiene factors – the need to avoid harm from the environment.	☐
Describe the managerial implications of applying Herzberg's theory in practice.	The implications of Herzberg's theory of motivation for the workplace include the following: • Employees that are dissatisfied cannot be motivated. • Managers need first to ensure that the hygiene factors are present to avoid staff becoming dissatisfied, before introducing the motivators. • Employees are motivated by work that allows them to make real achievements. • The achievements of employees need to be recognised. • The job itself needs to be designed in a manner that is exciting and challenging.	☐
Describe the concepts of 'expectancy' and 'valence' as used in Vroom's process theory of motivation.	The concepts of Vroom's expectancy theory include: • expectancy – an individual's expectation that a certain level of effort will lead to visible performance • instrumentality – the degree to which an individual believes that performing at a particular level will lead to the achievement of the desired outcome • valence – the degree to which organisational rewards satisfy an individual's personal goals or needs and the attractiveness of those potential rewards for the individuals.	☐
Describe the implications which the expectancy model of motivation has in organisations.	The implications of Vroom's theory of motivation for the workplace include the following: • Employees will be motivated to perform better if they believe that their efforts will lead to achievements that will satisfy their personal goals. • Managers need to realise that employees may place different values on the same reward. For example, some people may value the status of a job title (such as CEO) very highly, while for others their job title may be of much less importance. • Different employees may view the relationships between effort, performance and reward in different ways. For example, managers will need to be very clear when communicating the performance criteria and how these criteria relate to rewards. • Employees need to view performance standards as achievable. For example, managers may need to consult with employees to set reasonable and attainable targets that will be effective motivators. • Employees need adequate support, information and resources (such as equipment) to improve their performance.	☐

Explain how people are motivated according to Adams' equity theory of motivation by referring to inputs and outputs.	Adams' theory of fairness includes: • inputs – what employees put into the jobs • outputs – what benefits employees get out of the job • comparison process – how employees perceive their ratio of inputs and outputs to compare to the ratio of inputs and outputs of others.	☐
Discuss how inequity may be reduced by applying Adams' theory in practice.	Refer to Figure 1.13.	☐
Discuss and evaluate strategies for effective motivation in practice.	Strategies for effective motivation in practice include: • job design – the activities of job enlargement, job enrichment, job rotation, and job simplification • management by objectives (MBO) – management tool used to set goals and evaluate performance • productivity gain-sharing – incentive plan that encourages employees to work together to improve productivity.	☐

Assessment

1. True or false questions

Indicate whether the following statements are TRUE or FALSE. Write only 'true' or 'false' next to the question number.

1.1 Inequity arises when employees feel that they are being treated fairly.

1.2 Motivation has little effect on efficiency or productivity.

1.3 The motivation process is based on our desire to satisfy our needs.

1.4 Intrinsic motivation comes from something outside of yourself.

1.5 The term 'motivate' comes from the Latin word for 'move'.

1.6 Monetary rewards are an example of intrinsic motivators.

1.7 It is impossible for two people to have the same need and react in the same way.

1.8 Herzberg's theory recognises job security as a hygiene factor or dissatisfier.

1.9 Productivity gain-sharing is the same as profit sharing.

1.10 Adams' theory of fairness compares inputs to outputs.

(10 × 2)

[20]

2. Multiple-choice questions

Choose the correct answer from the various options provided. Write only A, B, C or D next to the question number.

2.1 Which of the following is a disadvantage of management by objectives (MBO)? (2)

    A Objectives can be used as performance standards.

    B Managers may lack understanding.

    C Employees are empowered.

    D Employees understand their role in the organisation.

2.2 Which of the following is not a motivator in Herzberg's theory? (2)

    A salary

    B achievement

    C praise

    D responsibility

2.3 Which two factors are Herzberg's motivational theory based on? (2)

    A hygiene factors and demotivators

    B motivation factors and satisfiers

    C hygiene factors and motivators

    D hygiene factors and dissatisfiers

2.4 Which of the following is not a component of Vroom's process theory? (2)

    A expectancy

    B outputs

    C instrumentality

    D valence

2.5 Which of the following is not a need that employees want to experience in their jobs to have a feeling of self-fulfilment and motivation? (2)

    A   need for achievement

    B   need for entertainment

    C   need for affiliation

    D   need for power

2.6 _____ is a step that employees can follow to maintain equity. (2)

    A   avoiding favouritism

    B   applying company rules consistently

    C   giving praise and recognition

    D   putting in less effort

2.7 Which of the following is not a method of job design? (2)

    A   job description

    B   job enlargement

    C   job enrichment

    D   job rotation

2.8 Which of the following is not a distinct part of the MBO process? (2)

    A   setting objectives

    B   sharing productivity gains

    C   encouraging employee participation

    D   evaluating employee performance

2.9 Which of the following is not a hygiene factor in Herzberg's theory? (2)

    A   salary

    B   service conditions

    C   personal growth

    D   job security

2.10 Which of the following is not a component of Maslow's hierarchy of needs? (2)

    A   psychological needs

    B   social needs

    C   physiological needs

    D   safety and security needs

(10 × 2)

[20]

3. Matching columns

Choose a phrase from COLUMN B that matches the term in COLUMN A. Write only the letter A, B, C, D or E next to the question number.

	Column A		Column B
3.1	Intrinsic motivation	A	a goal-setting technique
3.2	Management by objectives	B	factors outside the job
3.3	Job simplification	C	a desire to feel accepted by others
3.4	Extrinsic motivation	D	feelings of self-fulfilment and enjoyment
3.5	A need for affiliation	E	reducing the physical or mental effort required

(5 × 2)

[10]

4. Short questions

Answer the following short questions as thoroughly as possible.

4.1 Explain the following terms:

    4.1.1 job enrichment (2)

    4.1.2 productivity gain-sharing (2)

    4.1.3 job enlargement (2)

    4.1.4 job rotation (2)

4.2 Name two aspects of Adams' equity theory. (2)

[10]

5. Long questions

Answer the following questions in as much detail as possible.

5.1 Name and explain the three variables of Vroom's theory. (3 × 2)

5.2 What are the implications of Vroom's expectancy theory for an organisation? (4 × 1)

5.3 Explain the five needs of Maslow's hierarchy of needs with the aid of examples. (5 × 2)

5.4 Differentiate between intrinsic and extrinsic motivators and provide four examples of each motivator. (2 + 8)

5.5 Explain any five factors that will motivate employees in the workplace. (5 × 2)

5.6 Briefly explain the concept of management by objectives (MBO) and list four advantages of this motivational strategy. (5 × 2)

[50]

Total: [110]

COMMUNICATION

This module covers the following aspects of personnel management:

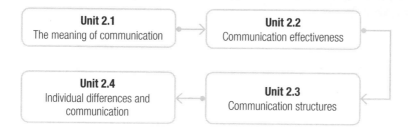

Unit 2.1
The meaning of communication

Unit 2.2
Communication effectiveness

Unit 2.4
Individual differences and communication

Unit 2.3
Communication structures

Learning objectives

When you have completed this module, you should be able to do the following:
- Describe the communication process in a pragmatic manner.
- Explain the importance of effective communication in the workplace.
- Describe communication barriers common to most enterprises.
- Outline techniques specifically developed for improving communication effectiveness.
- Describe the effect of organisational structures on effective communication referring to tall and flat organisational structures and staff and line organisations.
- Determine the nature and flow of information in communication through the effect of organisational level and status differences, organisational complexity, and communication networks.
- Define the difference between formal and informal communication channels in organisations.
- Explain how individual differences, such as gender differences, ethnicity and age; different values, attitudes and experiences; amount and type of education; and communication styles impact on communication behaviour.

Key terms

communication process
formal communication
communication barriers

informal communication
communication networks
organisational structures

communication styles

Starting point

Communication in the digital age

Most of us can remember that communication used to nearly always be face-to-face. Also, if not face-to-face, then a phone call on a telephone with a cord attached to the wall! Nowadays, information is mostly relayed online or electronically. Subsequently, most of the traditional ways to read and interpret communication messages now go lost in translation.

Figure 2.1 Communication in the digital age

Today, the receivers of our communication messages do not usually hear our voices and are consequently not able to read into the vocal tone; nor can Information Age communication receivers interpret your body language signals. Your original message may become completely misread, distorted and misunderstood.

On the flip side, our need to communicate effectively has never been higher! Humans operate technology. We still need to be understood, appreciated and communicated with professionally. Social media demands that people grow their ability to write skillfully. Your writing ability ultimately determines how you are perceived on the world social media stage.

Voice recognition is increasingly becoming a mandatory tool to communicate with each other and with the technology itself. I am sure you have witnessed people cursing 'Siri', the virtual voice recognition assistant on their cell phones, for misinterpreting their vocal commands. In reality, 90% of the time most cell phone users mumble and have week and obscure voices that cannot be understood either by technology nor other humans! The need to learn to speak clearly is becoming increasingly important.

Meetings and conferencing are also increasingly being conducted by Skype and video conferencing. Many professionals are currently self-sabotaging by demonstrating a lack of confidence and the inability to communicate effectively when using these media.

Communication in the digital age may have evolved dramatically, but the necessity for excellent communication skills remains the same. Communication skills are now even more critical, with cues like body language and vocal tone being cut out of the communication equation. Your remaining tools to communicate with now need to be leveraged with an even greater skill to compensate for the lack of face-to-face communication. In every era, communication skills triumph!

Source: Adapted from *Communication in the Digital Age*, J. French (26 September 2012). Available at https://www.entrepreneurmag.co.za/advice/growing-a-business/innovation/communication-in-the-digital-age/

UNIT 2.1 Meanings and definitions of communication

In Starting point, you saw how good communication skills remain a necessity in every organisation, even though the way we communicate may have changed over time. Communication is essential for people to understand each other and be able to work together. The Human Resources function aims to maintain the relationship between the organisation and its employees. To achieve this, the Personnel Manager will need to have excellent verbal and written communication skills.

> **Flashback to N4**: In Module 1 of *Succeed in Personnel Management N4* you learned how clear, effective and regular communication at all levels of an organisation is essential to its ultimate success.

Figure 2.2 The concept of communication

Power Break 2.1   INDIVIDUAL WORK

Define the concept of 'communication' logically in your own words.

2.1.1 The communication process

The communication process can be defined as a two-way process during which information is transmitted in specific code and using a specific channel or medium, from a sender to a receiver, who reacts to the stimulus using feedback. This two-way process of communication can be illustrated as a cycle, as follows:

Figure 2.3 A basic model of communication

The sender and receiver can use different channels to send the message and the feedback. Table 2.1 explains the various elements of the communication process in more detail.

Table 2.1 The communication process

Element	Explanation
Sender	The start of the communication process, or the source of communication; the person communicating or sending the message encodes the message.
Message	The information that is sent to the receiver. It is transmitted using a particular code, such as a language (a process known as **encoding**).
Channel/medium	The message is sent via a channel or a medium, for example, a letter, telephone or verbally.
Receiver	The person who receives the information, also known as the destination. This person pays close attention to the message to provide an adequate response (a process known as **decoding**).
Feedback	The response or the reaction of the receiver to the message. It can be conscious or unconscious, positive or negative, direct or indirect and verbal or non-verbal.
Noise	Can occur at any point in the communication process. Also known as interference or barriers to communication. It can cause the communication process to break down completely, for example, a stubborn person might not want to listen to the sender's ideas and stops listening, or a telephone conversation ends because one of the participants runs out of airtime.

Key point: The communication process is a two-way process during which information is transmitted in a specific code, via a specific channel or medium, from a sender to a receiver, who reacts to the message using feedback.

Power Break 2.2   INDIVIDUAL WORK

Read the following scenario carefully and then answer the questions that follow.

Esther is the Personnel Manager for a large company. The company's General Manager recently noticed a decrease in employee productivity and gave Esther the task of compiling a report to explain how this issue could be addressed. Esther spent all weekend researching and writing her report. While she was giving her presentation, the General Manager kept fidgeting and looking at his watch. Esther was busy explaining the benefits of team-building as a motivational strategy when the telephone rang.

continued on the next page …

DEFINITIONS

encodes – changes thoughts or ideas into language, letters, symbols, etc.

decodes – finds the meaning of something

The General Manager took the call, telling Esther that their time was up. Esther left her report on the General Managers desk and walked out.

1 Can you identify the sender, message, medium and receiver in this scenario?
2 What was the aim of this communication?
3 Was this communication successful? Give a reason for your answer.
4 Discuss the barriers or noise that affected this communication process.

2.1.2 The importance of effective communication in the workplace

Organisations are formed with the purpose of achieving a particular vision, mission, and particular objectives. For these goals to be attained, there must be clear and effective **interpersonal communication** between the various people working in the organisation.

Did you know? The main categories of communication are interpersonal (between people) and intrapersonal communication (with yourself). Mass communication is directed at large groups of people and takes place via the media, for example, television, radio, magazines and the internet.

The aims of internal communication are the following:
- Ensure a free flow of information at all levels within the organisation.
- Encourage effective two-way communication between management and employees.
- Help employees to understand the organisation's goals and their role in helping the organisation reach these goals.
- Improve productivity, cooperation and employee motivation levels.
- Maintain sound interpersonal relationships.
- Create and maintain a climate of openness and trust within the organisation.
- Minimise and resolve the conflict.
- Help employees realise that their success is linked to the organisation's success.

Key point: All organisations strive to achieve a healthy communication climate. Communication climate refers to the atmosphere of the communicative relationships between people in a workplace or living together. Information flows more freely in an organisation with a good communication climate.

Why is effective communication necessary in the world of work?
- It ensures fewer misunderstandings.
- Everyone knows exactly what is expected of them and how to accomplish tasks.

DEFINITION

interpersonal communication – connected with relationships between people

- It ensures greater teamwork and productivity.
- It leads to a more positive working environment.

There are, therefore, many advantages to effective communication. Effective communication:

- provides sensible feedback
- maintains sound interpersonal relationships
- motivates, encourages and persuades co-workers towards achieving specific goals
- considers problems logically and solves them
- minimises and resolves conflict
- ensures effective teamwork and group discussions
- ensures that the objectives of the organisation are achieved.

Example 2.1

A company such as Woolworths clearly states on its website that it is 'committed to engaging with all employees formally and informally on a regular basis ensuring that employees remain informed of key business issues and developments'.

Source: http://www.woolworthsholdings.co.za/investor/annual_reports/ar2006/sr/social.asp

Employees that are well informed are more confident and committed to the organisation's goals and are happy to promote the organisation in more favourable terms. Everyone likes to enjoy their work and be happy at his or her place of work.

Conversely, an employee who lacks good communication skills could negatively affect the organisation that they work for in the long term. The Personnel Manager will need to pay close attention to those aspects of employer-employee communication that could lead to disputes and even strikes. Poor communication could result in dissatisfied customers, unhappy employers, low productivity, poor service, and ultimately, a decrease in sales and revenue.

Power Break 2.3 GROUP WORK

1 Look carefully at the pictures shown above. Work in your groups to discuss each scene. Which of these scenes shows a healthy communication climate and which does not? Give reasons for your answers.
2 Create a list of the characteristics that you think would be necessary to ensure a healthy, positive communication climate in an organisation. Share your group's answers with the class.

UNIT 2.2 **Communication effectiveness**

Effective communication can minimise conflict and can prevent misunderstandings. Whenever you have to interact with other people, you will benefit from knowing communication skills. However, effective communication is about more than just sharing information with someone. For communication to be effective there needs to be a match between what you planned to say, what you said, and what your audience interpreted!

One of the ways in which you can improve your communication skills is by learning to recognise and reduce the effects of 'noise' or interferences on the communication process.

2.2.1 Communication barriers common to most enterprises

A communication barrier can be defined as any factor that prevents the message between the sender and the receiver from being delivered effectively. Barriers cause a breakdown in the communication process and are also known as noise or interference.

Barriers can be found at any point in the communication process and could be the result of either external or internal factors. The most common types of barriers include external barriers, known as physical barriers, and internal barriers, which include physiological, psychological, perceptual, prejudice, stereotyping, ethnocentricity and semantic barriers.

Figure 2.4 Barriers prevent the message from being delivered effectively.

Table 2.2 explains some of the most prominent barriers to interpersonal communication and social interaction.

Table 2.2 Communication barriers

Factor	Explanation
Physical (environmental) barriers	External or physical barriers are factors outside the sender and the receiver that cause a message to be delivered ineffectively or not at all. For example, it would be difficult to have an effective conversation with someone where there are loud background noises, when using a cell phone with a weak signal, or when they are in a different time zone.
Physiological barriers	A physiological barrier occurs when the health condition of either the sender or receiver causes the communication process to be ineffective. For example, having poor hearing or eyesight can make spoken or written communication more difficult.
Psychological (attitudinal) barriers	A psychological barrier occurs when certain personality traits, emotions or the mental condition of either the sender or the receiver cause the communication process to be ineffective. It can also be the result of a lack of credibility or negative attitude in the sender or receiver. For example, a person who is very shy may have difficulty giving a speech.
Semantic (language) barriers	A semantic barrier occurs when the sender understands a word differently or attaches a different meaning to a word than the receiver (or vice versa). The receiver might misinterpret the message, causing misunderstandings or even offence. Examples of semantic barriers include: using **ambiguous** or vague expressions, speaking in **slang**, using **jargon**, pronouncing words with a particular accent, etc.
Perceptual barriers	Perceptual barriers occur when the sender and the receiver differ in their **perceptions**, norms and values, causing the communication process to be ineffective. Perceptual barriers can be caused by differences in culture, attitude, background, age, education and training, interests, needs, occupation, personality, religion, gender, etc.
Prejudice, stereotyping and ethnocentricity	Prejudice, stereotyping and ethnocentricity lead to psychological barriers as well as perceptual barriers, which could render the communication process ineffective. • A prejudice is an unfair and unreasonable opinion, usually formed without enough prior thought or knowledge. For example, a person might have negative feelings towards a colleague before getting to know him or her. • Stereotyping means attaching specific characteristics to a person just because they belong to a particular group. For example, an older manager may believe that all young employees are disrespectful. • Ethnocentricity (also known as a multicultural barrier) is the belief that your own culture is superior to any other culture or ethnic group. For example, a Western manager conducting an interview may judge an African interviewee negatively because he or she does not make eye contact.

DEFINITIONS

ambiguous – having more than one meaning

slang – the informal language used and understood by a specific social group

jargon – words or expressions used by a particular profession or group

perceptions – ideas or beliefs that you have as the result of how you see something

Example 2.2

In Starting point, you saw how the use of technology to relay information online or electronically had created more communication barriers. Without appropriate cues such as body language or vocal tone, it is easier for your original message to become completely misread, distorted and misunderstood.

Figure 2.5 Poor communication can cause misunderstandings in the workplace.

Power Break 2.4   INDIVIDUAL WORK

continued on the next page …

1. Read the dialogue above and identify examples of each of the specific barriers that could harm the communication process between the employer and the employee.
   a) Psychological barrier
   b) Physiological barrier
   c) Perceptual barrier: age
   d) Perceptual barrier: needs
   e) Perceptual barrier: interests
   f) Stereotyping
2. Study the young female and male colleague and identify two specific barriers that could harm the communication process between a man and a woman.
3. Think of the relationship that you have with your parents. Identify two specific barriers that could damage the communication process between a parent and child.

Did you know? People may intentionally create communication barriers because they fear the consequences of their actions. This process is known as gatekeeping. For example, an employee might avoid contact with their manager because they haven't completed a task that was due on that day.

2.2.2 Techniques developed for improving communication effectiveness

For internal employee communication to be effective, organisations need to be aware of and follow certain principles (guidelines or rules) that will ensure success. Individual employees also need to consider how they can improve their communication skills.

Employees can improve their interpersonal communications by:
- selecting the most appropriate communication channel for each particular situation
- speaking clearly and loudly enough
- listening well
- using plain and straightforward language that is not vague
- being sensitive to the receiver's background; taking into account their culture, age, needs, interests, and level of intelligence
- using tact when giving criticism and accepting constructive criticism without being defensive.

Organisations can use the following principles of employee communication as guidelines:
- Have a clear communication strategy/plan which is revised annually.
- Ensure that top management participates in and supports the communication plan.
- Put into place proper channels of communication.
- Ensure secure and direct access to different means of communication.
- Deliver relevant information **timeously** and avoid filtering out negative news.

> **DEFINITION**
>
> **timeously** – in good time; early enough

- Ensure that there are channels and opportunities for feedback.
- There must be a two-way flow of information, for example from management to supervisors to employees and from employees to supervisors to management.
- Respect all employees. Keep in mind that in South Africa we have a **diverse** culture and employees come from different cultural backgrounds.
- Keep employees well informed of important events or changes that may affect them.
- Monitor and regularly evaluate the communication strategy.

> **Key point:** All business communication, whether written or spoken, should be clear and to the point.

Once a good communication strategy is in place, it is important to monitor it with the aim of maintaining and improving where necessary. Many organisations conduct internal communication audits either annually or bi-annually to determine how well their communication programmes meet the needs of their employees. They do this through questionnaires, surveys, meetings, interviews, and feedback from staff.

Figure 2.6 Using a communication satisfaction questionnaire as a communication audit tool

The first step in evaluating the effectiveness of the communication strategy is to gather information about the current communication system. Use a survey to collect information from employees regarding the current system's efficiency. Here are examples of some of the questions that you could ask employees to gather information about the current communication climate within the organisation:
- Does the current system work for you?
- Are you happy with it?
- What do you think about communication within the organisation?
- What is your opinion about management?

> **DEFINITION**
>
> **diverse** – very different from each other, for example, different literacy levels, backgrounds, cultures, language differences, etc.

- Do you think you are kept well informed?
- Are you getting the information that you want?
- Are sufficient channels for communication and feedback provided?
- Are the channels that are in place working effectively for you?
- Do you have any suggestions/recommendations for improvement?

Once you have gathered information from the surveys or questionnaires, evaluate employee responses. Then, taking the responses into account, revise or upgrade the current plan if necessary. Share the new plan with all employees and implement it.

Power Break 2.5 GROUP WORK

'Broken telephone' is a popular party game that illustrates how communication barriers can prevent a message from being delivered effectively. Each group must select a group leader who is tasked with writing down a phrase or sentence that the other group members have not yet heard or seen. The group leader must whisper this message into the ear of another member, who in turn must repeat it to somebody else in the group. When the last person in the group has heard the message, they must write it down.

1 Was your group able to successfully transfer the group leader's original message?
2 Discuss the factors that may have negatively affected the communication process. Now select a new group leader and repeat the activity with a different phrase.
3 Was this communication more effective than your group's first attempt?
4 Do you think that repeating the activity would further improve communications between your group members? Give reasons for your answer.

UNIT 2.3 Communication structures

The formal arrangement of jobs is referred to as the business's organisational structure. The communication structure of an organisation is the formal representation of how information flows within an organisation. We use organisational charts (organograms) to illustrate the organisation's communication structure and the flow of information from one person or department to the next. Figure 2.7 provides an example of this.

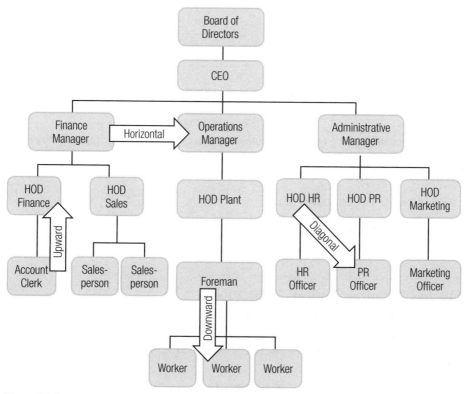

Figure 2.7 An example of a total company communication structure

Flashback to N4: In Module 2 of *Succeed in Personnel Management N4* you learned how the personnel department plays a key role in setting up and informing organisational structure, by providing senior management with information about the organisational structure that they need.

2.3.1 Effect of organisational structures on effective communication

The organisational structure clearly shows how the different roles, responsibilities and power are assigned to positions in the business. Organisational charts also illustrate the way these lines of authority are structured (such as line or staff) and indicate how information and instructions will flow between the different levels of management. When creating an organisational structure, you will need to make sure that it contains the information in Table 2.3

Table 2.3 Components of an organisational structure

Factor	Description
The division of work	Every position in the organisation must be represented separately in the structure.
The nature of the work	Positions should be grouped into appropriate departments according to the type of work that is performed.
Chain of command	Clear reporting lines, flowing from the top of the business down, must indicate who is in charge of what activities.
Unity of command	Each position must only report to one supervisor to ensure a clear reporting relationship.
The levels of management	The structure should indicate which positions form part of the top, middle or lower management.
The span of control	The structure must show how many positions report to each manager.

Power Break 2.6 GROUP WORK

Take a look at the organisational structure depicted in Figure 2.7. Does this organogram meet all the requirements that are listed in Table 2.3?

Tall and flat organisational structures

The type of organisational structure that a business chooses will depend on the type of industry that it operates in, the amount of control that managers need to have over the employees, and the organisation's overall objectives and strategy. Table 2.4 illustrates two of the most common types of structure.

A tall organisational structure is often referred to as a pyramid-type organisation as there are a relatively high number of levels in its hierarchy of authority. These extra levels make the lines of communication very long. Messages can take time to flow from management to employees and vice versa. It makes it harder for the organisation to adapt to changes or respond quickly in a crisis. The high number of levels also increases the risk of the message becoming distorted as it is relayed from one level to the next. For example, workers may threaten to strike if they believe that their supervisors are not accurately conveying their grievances to top management.

Organisational rules and policies can also influence the effectiveness of communication. Organisations with a tall structure tend to have stricter rules and policies. For example, the organisation's communication policy may stipulate that all communication should be done in writing. It means that even the most straightforward message would need to be written down. It delays the communication process and subsequently, managers' decision-making.

Table 2.4 Different types of organisational structures

Tall (traditional or bureaucratic) structure	Flat structure

• Has many different levels of management and each manager only supervises a few workers. • Results in rigid control with well-defined regulations, rules and policies.	• Has fewer levels of management, each manager may supervise many workers. • Control is less rigid because employees are expected to work independently.
• Examples: most government departments, banks, large organisations.	• Examples: smaller organisations, law firms, creative agencies, scientists, IT specialists.

I THINK WE HAVE A COMMUNICATION PROBLEM!

YOU CAN SAY THAT AGAIN... I FIRED YOU TWO WEEKS AGO!

Figure 2.8 Communication may be slower in a tall organisational structure.

In comparison, a flat organisational structure has less middle-management levels. It brings the top management in direct contact with customers or **frontline employees** such as salespeople. In a flat organisation, messages and feedback can travel more quickly. It means that managers can respond to changing conditions or customer needs much faster. A disadvantage of this structure is that employees may not receive enough support or guidance since each manager has a wide span of control with many

DEFINITION

frontline employees – employees who deal directly with customers or the public

subordinates to communicate with. Organisations with a flat structure must ensure that managers have adequate facilities (such as email or telephone networks) through which to communicate messages timeously and effectively.

Line and staff organisational structures

Authority means having the power or right to do something, or to give orders to others to get it done. The lines of authority in the organisational structure can influence the way in which important messages, such as instructions or feedback, are communicated within the organisation.

Line structure is the simplest and most common form of organisational structure. Line structure is hierarchical, which means authority starts at the top and moves downward. In a company with line organisational structure, each departmental manager has control over his or her departmental affairs. Line managers have the authority to delegate tasks directly to their employees, making communication faster and more efficient.

Example 2.3

Sheryl is the Sales Manager in a medical insurance company. She holds daily meetings with her team of sales representatives to discuss their progress towards achieving monthly targets. By communicating directly with her team, Sheryl can get immediate feedback about issues which may affect the efficiency of the sales department.

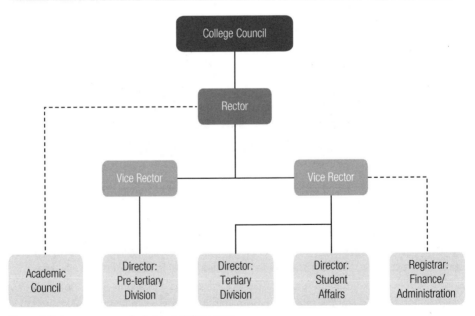

Figure 2.9 An organogram of a line and staff structure

This structure is a line organisation, but it is a little more complicated. It consists of a line structure in which individual staff members have particular knowledge or skills to share, yet they do not have any authority to make decisions. A staff member who has specific skills can assist senior staff members. Thus, it is known as a line and staff organisation.

It is made up of supervisors and assistants. An employee can advise his or her senior on some issues but cannot make any big decisions that would impact the company. For example, a secretary might reorganise her senior's schedule so that he or she has more time to prioritise other pressing issues.

Table 2.5 Advantages and disadvantages of a line and staff organisation

Advantages	Disadvantages
• The advice and skills of individual staff members can relieve the work of seniors. • There is better coordination through specialisation and better decision-making. • The staff members who have special skills can train other staff members. • It allows for effective control and unity within the company.	• It can create confusion as some staff members might feel overlooked and that their skills are lacking. • The senior might get used to relying on staff to make decisions. • Senior staff members might resent an employee if he or she shows a higher level of competency.

When the organisation grows, and managers are not able to handle all their tasks efficiently, the organisational structure may be changed to line and staff. In a line and staff organisational structure, other employees are hired to help line managers and perform activities they do not have time to get to. Line functions are those that contribute directly to company profits, including production managers or sales representatives. Staff functions are those that provide support to line functions, such as legal, human resources and public relations.

Flashback to N4: In Module 2 of *Succeed in Personnel Management N4* you learned how to illustrate the line and staff organisational structures using an organisational chart (organogram).

The authority of staff managers is limited to making recommendations to line managers. Having both line and staff functions often cause conflict or confusion among employees. For example, line managers may not trust the advice that they are being given and staff managers may **overstep** their limited authority. If the lines of authority are not clear, employees will not know whose instructions they should follow! A detailed communication structure with clear chains of command is essential for line and staff functions to work together effectively.

Key point: Tall organisations that have both line and staff functions usually have a more formal communication structure, while flat organisations with only line functions may communicate more informally.

DEFINITION

overstep – to go beyond what is normal or allowed

2.3.2 Nature and flow of information in communication

Many different factors can affect the flow of information within an organisation. These include the hierarchical positions that exist in the organisation, how complex the organisational structure is, and what type of communication networks are used within the organisation.

Organisational level and status differences	Organisational complexity	Communication networks

Figure 2.10 Factors affecting the nature and flow of information in communication

Organisational level and status differences

Most organisational structures have many employees at each of the various organisational levels (e.g. top, middle and lower). Each employee's position in the structure also has a different status or rank in comparison to other people in the organisation. An organisation's communication structure shows how information flows from one level or rank to another.

Formal internal communication may flow through various routes: vertical (upward and downward), horizontal or diagonal. These different routes can be seen in figure 2.7.

Downward communication ⬇

- Information flows from upper levels to lower levels, following the hierarchical structure, for example from the Foreman to a worker.
- Includes job instructions, feedback on performance, strategic plans, organisation's policies, mission, values and goals, meetings, disciplinary procedures, workshops, memos and notices.

Upward communication ⬆

- Information flows from lower to higher levels within the organisation, for example from the accounts clerk to the HOD of Finance.
- Includes reports, proposals, grievance procedures, feedback, suggestions and queries.

Horizontal communication ➡

- Takes place across departments, between people on the same level, for example, an email from the Marketing officer to the PR officer.
- Includes interdepartmental meetings, memos, peer groups and task groups

Diagonal communication ↘

- Takes place across different departments and different levels of authority, for example, the Human Resources Manager discussing an issue with the PR officer.
- This method of communication tends to bypass the standard chain of command and can take place through various channels.

> **Did you know?** An employee's organisational level or status can create a communication barrier. For example, top-level managers may be less inclined to listen to the feedback from lower level workers if they believe that the workers are inferior because of their lower status.

Organisational complexity

The flow of information is also affected by organisational **complexity**. A complicated organisational structure can make effective communication more difficult. There is a greater chance of information being distorted when the lines of communication are long, and information has to flow between many different people on different levels. Complexity also refers to how organisations are made up of many different parts, such as the different functional departments, which all need to communicate with each other and work together to achieve the organisation's overall objectives and vision.

> **Key point:** Organisations that are less hierarchical have better upward and downward communication. Fewer levels mean fewer miscommunication opportunities.

An organisation's use of technology and its choice of communication channels will also affect the complexity of the communication structure. Communication technology is rapidly advancing and newer communication channels, such as instant messaging or social media, are becoming more commonly used in organisations. The preferred channels of communication must be specified in the communication policy. It prevents employees from selecting a channel that is inappropriate for the intended audience. Some employees will find it challenging to adapt to these new methods and may require additional training before they can use technology to communicate effectively.

Figure 2.11 Having too many communication channels can be confusing.

DEFINITION

complexity – being formed of many parts; difficult to understand

---

Power Break 2.7 GROUP ACTIVITY

Assign a group member to visit the various departments at your college to gather information about its organisational structure. Try to learn what functions are performed by each department and which positions are allocated to its staff members. Use the information to complete the following:

1 Draw an organogram showing the organisational structure of your college. Include as many of the different departments and specific job positions as you can.
2 Now use the organogram to answer the following questions:
   a) What type of organisational structure does your college have? Motivate your answer.
   b) Can you identify a specific position that represents each of the top, middle and lower levels of management?
   c) Provide an example of how communication could flow through each of the four formal routes: upward, downward, horizontal and diagonal.
   d) List the various channels that your college uses for communication.
   e) In your opinion, does the organisational structure of your college allow for effective communication? If not, what would you change to allow for better functioning?

Communication networks

Information can flow in different patterns, depending on how the senders and receivers are arranged. These patterns are called communication networks. Different types of networks are effective in different situations. The choice of communication network usually depends on the particular tasks or goals that a department, group or team are trying to accomplish. It is because communication networks can affect how fast messages travel and how accurately information is relayed.

Did you know? Most organisations have both formal and informal communication networks. You will learn more about the formal and informal communication channels later in this unit.

Communication networks can be centralised or decentralised. In a centralised network, all communications are controlled by one particular employee, who takes the lead and directs the flow of information. Centralised networks are very effective when employees need to accomplish simple tasks efficiently and consistently. The main disadvantage of the centralised network is that individual employees are isolated from others, so messages can take a long time to flow throughout the network. Some employees may also become demotivated because they cannot participate fully in the communication process.

Figure 2.12 shows how communication flows in centralised networks.

Chain network

- Information flows upwards and downwards along the chain.
- Each employee receives information from their immediate superior and passes it along to their immediate subordinates.
- Each employee is connected to the creator of the chain (A).

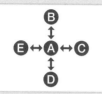

Wheel network

- This is the most centralised type of network.
- All information flows from one central employee (A).
- Communication between the other employees is either very limited or non-existent.

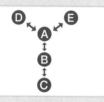

Y-network

- This is a modified version of the chain network, where two employees (D and E) are outside of the chain.
- Information flows from employees (D) and (E) through employee (A) to reach employees (B) and (C).

Figure 2.12 Centralised forms of communication networks

Decentralised communication networks are not controlled or lead by any particular employee. Information flows freely between most, or all, of the employees in the network. Decentralised networks are effective when employees need to solve complex problems or perform a wide variety of tasks. Being included in discussions and decision-making can improve employee motivation. However, the risk of employees receiving distorted or conflicting messages also increases.

Figure 2.13 shows how communication flows in decentralised networks.

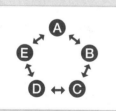

Circle network

- Each employee can communicate with two other employees in the network.
- There is no leader to direct the flow of communication.
- For example, employee (A) can share information with employee (B) and (E) but has to go through employee (B) to communicate with employee (C).

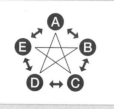

All-channel network

- This is the most decentralised type of network.
- All employees are connected, and information flows freely from anywhere in the organisation.
- For example, employee (A) can communicate with employees (E) and (B), but also with employees (D) and (C).

Figure 2.13 Decentralised forms of communication networks

2.3.3 Difference between formal and informal communication channels in organisations

To ensure a free flow of information, organisations use both formal and informal communication channels. Formal communication follows official channels. Examples include meetings, minutes of meetings, notices and reports. Informal communication usually supplements the official channels. Figure 2.14 explains the difference between formal and informal communication channels.

Formal communication

- is pre-determined by company rules, procedures and policies
- is also known as official communication
- follows a **hierarchical** chain of command
- is mostly written
- is more time-consuming
- is more reliable.

Informal communication

- does not follow any particular guidelines
- is also known as the **grapevine**
- moves freely in all directions and is very quick
- is not always reliable because information can get **distorted** as it runs via different channels from one person to the other
- includes casual discussions, rumours and gossip
- is mostly oral, but can consist of social networking applications such as WhatsApp, Twitter and Facebook.

Figure 2.14 The characteristics of formal and informal communication channels

---

Flashback to N4: In Module 2 of *Succeed in Personnel Management N4* you learned about the advantages and disadvantages of the informal organisation structure, which operates within the formal organisation structure.

Did you know? The grapevine is not always popular with management since it can negatively distort important company information. However, the advantage of the grapevine is that it can be used by management to gather information about staff motivation levels and opinions informally.

DEFINITIONS

hierarchical – when people are organised from the most to least powerful

grapevine – the circulation of rumours and unofficial information

distorted – to change the shape or sound of something so that it is no longer clear

*"I want everybody to know about this -
whisper it to Miss Tonks in Accounts."*

Figure 2.15 Information can be shared informally through the grapevine.

Power Break 2.8 INDIVIDUAL WORK

Identify which is an example of formal communication and which is an example of informal communication.

1 A meeting is held between departmental managers to discuss the launch of a new product.
2 A group of four employees meets for coffee in the cafeteria to plan a colleague's baby shower.
3 A rumour that the CEO has resigned and is moving to another country.
4 A notice warning staff to ensure that they follow specific safety procedures at all times.
5 The HR manager and the Production manager have a chat about a staff issue while walking to their cars.

Key point: Managers can reduce employees' reliance on the grapevine by using formal communication more frequently. If employees expect to receive an official version, they will be less inclined to believe rumours.

UNIT 2.4 Individual differences and communication

Once a message has been received, it needs to be interpreted. It means that the receiver adds their meaning to what is being said. The individual differences that are found among people in an organisation can have a significant impact on their communication behaviour and thus communication effectiveness.

2.4.1 Gender differences, ethnicity and age

Gender differences

Different genders may interpret and respond to messages differently. Very generally speaking, women may be more sympathetic and empathetic at work while men may be less so. The way in which different genders communicate with each other can be based on cultural and religious factors as well, and both men and women should be conscious of the potential bias they have when communicating.

> **Key point:** Gender differences are based mainly on generalisations. It is important that you do not make assumptions about people's behaviour just because they are male or female.

Ethnic differences

Your ethnicity refers to the particular cultural group that you identify yourself as belonging to. Different ethnic groups follow different practices and often perceive the same things in different ways. Different value systems also guide them. In South Africa, our cultural and ethnic diversity means that we interact and communicate with people from many different backgrounds. It is therefore vital that we learn to respect different cultural approaches to avoid offending. For example, a particular phrase of speech or non-verbal cue that seems polite in one culture may appear as an insult in another culture.

> **Key point:** Cultural relativity means that what is acceptable behaviour in one culture may not be acceptable in another.

For communication to be effective, the ethnicity of the receiver should be taken into consideration when encoding the message, choosing the communication channel, and analysing the feedback. People from various ethnic groups may attach different meanings to particular words or terms, use a different volume or tone of voice, have a different preference for eye contact, or use more or less body language. The sender of the message will need to keep all of these variances in mind and pay particular attention to the feedback to ensure that the receiver correctly decoded the message.

Figure 2.16 Understanding cultural norms can improve your communication.

Did you know? In some cultures, too much eye contact is seen as rude or threatening. In others, too little is seen as impolite or untrustworthy.

Unlike South Africans, many Asian cultures do not gesture or speak with their hands as they find it distracting.

The loudness of voice indicates strength in Arabic cultures, but in some Asian cultures, it may mean a loss of control or show impoliteness.

Power Break 2.9 GROUP WORK

1 Work in your groups to discuss the various ways in which ethnic differences may affect the communication process and lead to misunderstandings in the workplace.
2 Pair up with a partner in your group and select one of the scenarios to role-play in front of the class.
3 Have a class discussion on how Personnel Managers can use **intercultural** training to improve cross-cultural communication in the workplace.

Age differences

Over the years, there have been many changes to how organisations operate. For example, young people are entering the workforce earlier, and many older people are retiring later. It means that the range of age groups found in the workplace is expanding.

> **DEFINITION**
>
> **intercultural** – existing or happening between different cultures

Conflict often arises between employees from different generational groups, as each generation may be accustomed to communicating differently.

Employees from the older generations may prefer to use more traditional communication channels such as memorandums, emails or face-to-face meetings. Younger employees are more likely to communicate using instant messaging, texting, social networking and video conferencing. Some older employees may resist adapting to technological changes and then become frustrated when they are 'left out of the loop'. Younger employees may find it difficult to communicate with older colleagues who don't understand their use of jargon or slang.

"I'm not used to communicating face-to-face. Can we conduct this interview via text?"

Figure 2.17 Age can affect communication preferences.

Did you know? Most organisations have employees that were born in at least four different generational groups: Generation Z (the 1990s), Generation Y (the 1980s), Generation X (the 1970s), and baby boomers (the 1960s).

2.4.2 Differences in values, attitudes and experience

People come from different walks of life. They have unique backgrounds with different values, education, race, upbringing, religious beliefs, culture, etc. People's attitudes also differ. They have different attitudes towards their jobs, tasks, responsibilities and their general outlook on life. It means that every person has a unique frame of reference that influences the way he or she perceives the world. Our frame of reference also evolves and changes throughout our lives.

Example 2.4

The staff of a large company often arrive late for work because of taxi strikes that delay their transport. Luckily, the manager remembers his days as a student and having to rely on public transport, so he has a similar frame of reference and thus is more understanding.

Whenever people differ, the possibility of misunderstanding exists. Communication skills must be flexible enough to accommodate many different kinds of people. You will need to be aware of your frame of reference and how this can impact on your communication with others. It would help if you also tried to learn more about the cultures and backgrounds of other people.

2.4.3 Amount and type of education

People come from different educational backgrounds. They have different abilities, knowledge of different subjects and they might use their jargon (**vocabulary**). For example, someone who studied accounting at school might find it easy to give a budget presentation at work while someone who didn't study accounting might find explaining budgets quite difficult.

Being well educated should make your communication more effective since it is expected that an educated person would have advanced writing and speaking skills, a bigger vocabulary and highly developed interpersonal skills.

2.4.4 Communication styles

Different people use different styles to communicate. The communication style you use can vary according to your personality and the situation you find yourself in. Some styles are more successful than others in the business environment. Table 2.6 discusses some of the different communication styles and outlines the situations where these particular styles may be of use in the workplace.

Table 2.6 Communication styles

Style	Characteristics	Technique	Situation
Controlling	Aggressive, poor listener. Has difficulty seeing the other person's point of view. Domineering, bossy, can be intimidating. Achieves goals.	Use of power and **manipulation**. One-way communication. Uses **monopolisation**, interruption and demanding techniques to get the message across.	Used in situations where people need to be directed, or quick decisions need to be made, e.g. military-style situations.

continued on the next page …

> **DEFINITIONS**
>
> **vocabulary** – all the words that a person knows or uses
>
> **manipulation** – a technique of influencing or forcing someone to do what you want
>
> **monopolisation** – a way of controlling or owning something; having complete control

Style	Characteristics	Technique	Situation
Egalitarian	Shows concern for others; encourages people to express their opinions and share ideas, attentive listener.	Facilitates two-way communication and active listening. Encourages feedback. Uses direct eye-contact.	Used when teamwork is involved and when cooperation is needed. Useful in problem-solving situations.
Structural	Sticks to the rules and procedures. Likes to organise and have structures in place. Uses organisational procedures to make a decision.	Issuing orders and assigning tasks. Relies mainly on oral or written communication. Is goal-oriented.	Used when a group/department/team is required to complete a specific task, especially when deadlines are involved.
Dynamic	High-energy, inspirational, practical, a 'doer', confident, decisive.	Direct; action-orientated. Focuses immediately on what needs to be done. Uses motivation techniques to get people to take action.	Useful in situations where a team needs to be motivated to carry out a task or in crises, but only when the receiver has the ability or knowledge required to perform the task.
Relinquishing	Non-judgemental, helpful, happy to shift responsibility, willing to let someone else find a solution to the problem, supportive, trusting.	Indirect; **deferential**; willing to let others assume responsibility.	Useful in supportive situations where no judgements are made, such as counselling or when a senior is advising a junior/intern.
Withdrawal	Self-conscious, passive, reluctant participant, not a team player, can be shy or have low self-esteem.	Use of silence, avoidance, withdrawal techniques. Uninvolved. Takes a neutral stance.	Occurs in situations where a person is disinterested in continuing the communication process, walks away, refuses to talk, avoids **confrontational** situations, and is unwilling to participate further.

> **DEFINITIONS**
>
> **deferential** – to be respectful towards something or somebody
>
> **confrontational** – to be in a tense or unpleasant situation that you must face

Power Break 2.10 INDIVIDUAL WORK

1 Identify the communication style used in the statements below:
   a) 'What are our options? 'What alternatives do we have?'
   b) 'Don't ask why. Just do it!'
   c) 'You do it; you have more experience than I do.'
2 Indicate which communication style would best fit each situation below:
   a) A supervisor gives urgent instructions to the workers in her department to sort out an unexpected crisis.
   b) The Financial Manager says: 'I have had a long day. I am tired of sorting out everyone's problems. I do not want to discuss it anymore.' (Walks out of the room)
   c) The head of the Human Resources department says to his staff: 'Okay people we have to sort this out by the end of the day. What do the rules say?'

Figure 2.18 A dynamic communication style will result in inspirational, practical, confident and decisive team players.

What have we learned about Personnel Management and where to next?

In this module, we learned about communication. We started by discussing the communication process and the importance of effective communication in the workplace. We went on to discuss the communication barriers and the techniques for improving communication effectiveness. Lastly, we looked at the communication structures and how individual differences can have an impact on communication behaviour.

In the next module, we will learn about group dynamics.

Revisiting the learning objectives

Now that you have completed this module let's see if you have achieved the learning outcomes that were set out at the beginning of the module. In the table below, we summarise what you have learned for each objective.

Learning objective	What have you learned	✓
Describe the communication process in a pragmatic manner.	The communication process has the following characteristics: • Effective communication is a two-way process. • Information is transmitted in a specific code. • Via a specific channel or medium. • From a sender to a receiver. • The reaction takes place using feedback. • Noise or interferences can occur at any point.	☐
Explain the importance of effective communication in the workplace.	Internal communication is important because it: • ensures a free flow of information at all levels within the organisation • encourages effective two-way communication between management and employees • helps employees to understand the organisation's goals and their role in helping the organisation reach these goals • improves productivity, cooperation, and employee motivation levels • maintains sound interpersonal relationships • creates and maintains a climate of openness and trust within the organisation • minimises and resolves conflict • helps employees realise that their success is linked to the organisation's success.	☐
Describe communication barriers common to most enterprises.	Refer to Table 2.2.	☐

Outline techniques developed explicitly for improving communication effectiveness.	Communication effectiveness can be improved by: • having a clear communication strategy/plan which is revised annually • ensuring that top management participates in and supports the communication plan • putting into place proper channels of communication • providing easy and direct access to different means of communication • delivering relevant information timeously and avoiding filtering of negative news • ensuring that there are channels and opportunities for feedback • having a two-way flow of information, for example from management to supervisors to employees and from employees to supervisors to management • respecting all employees • keeping employees well informed of important events or changes that may affect them • monitoring and regularly evaluating the communication strategy.
Describe the effect of organisational structures on effective communication.	Organisational structures affect how information and instructions flow between the different levels of management. The types of organisational structure include: • tall and flat organisational structures • line and staff organisational structures.
Determine the nature and flow of information in communication through the effect of organisational level and status differences, organisational complexity, and communication networks.	Formal internal communication routes include: • vertical (upward and downward) communication • horizontal communication • diagonal communication. Communication networks include: • chain network • wheel network • Y-network • circle network • all-channel network
Define the difference between formal and informal communication channels in organisations.	Refer to Figure 2.14.
Explain how individual differences impact on communication behaviour.	Communication behaviour can be affected by differences in: • gender, ethnicity and age • values, attitudes and experiences • amount and type of education • communication styles.

Assessment

1. True or false questions

Indicate whether the following statements are TRUE or FALSE. Write only 'true' or 'false' next to the question number.

1.1 Instructions and explanations should be as complicated as possible.

1.2 Individuals with lower education levels may become frustrated and withdraw from the communication process.

1.3 Effective communication is circular in nature.

1.4 The sender is the person who decodes the message.

1.5 Communication is essential for the effective running of any organisation.

1.6 Internal communication minimises and reduces conflict.

1.7 Communication can flow vertically, horizontally or diagonally.

1.8 Intrapersonal communication happens between people.

1.9 The flat organisational structure has fewer levels of management.

1.10 The wheel network is an example of decentralised communication.

(10 × 2)

[20]

2. Multiple-choice questions

Choose the correct answer from the various options provided. Write only A, B, C or D next to the question number.

2.1 Which of the following is not a component of organisational structures? (2)

    A unity of command

    B span of control

    C levels of management

    D organisational complexity

2.2 Which of the following is an example of a physical communication barrier? (2)

    A slang and jargon

    B loud background noises

    C ethnocentricity

    D poor hearing or eyesight

2.3 Informal structure referring to the fastest channel of communication. (2)

    A email

    B organogram

    C grapevine

    D meetings

2.4 Which of the following is not a technique for improving communication? (2)

    A using complex language

    B listening well

    C speaking clearly

    D accepting constructive criticism

2.5 Which of the following is not an example of a communication style? (2)

    A controlling

    B semantic

    C egalitarian

    D relinquishing

(5 × 2)
[10]

3. Matching columns

Match the correct term in Column B with the description in Column A.

	Column A		Column B
3.1	response or reaction	A	message
3.2	interferences or barriers	B	feedback
3.3	emails, telephone calls, meetings	C	noise
3.4	words, signs and symbols	D	receiver
3.5	decodes or interprets the message	E	channel

(5 × 2)
[10]

4. Short questions

Answer the following short questions as thoroughly as possible.

4.1 Explain the following terms:

    4.1.1 encoding (2)

    4.1.2 stereotyping (2)

4.2 Name three directions of communication flow. (3 x 1)

4.3 Name three types of centralised communication networks. (3 x 1)

[10]

5. Long questions

Answer the following questions in as much detail as possible.

5.1 Describe the process of communication in detail. (6 × 1)

5.2 Discuss the impact of education on communication. (4 × 1)

5.3 Discuss ten methods that managers could use to make communication more effective. (10 × 2)

5.4 Discuss five reasons why communication is important in the workplace. (5 × 2)

5.5 List ten factors that act as barriers to good communication. (10 × 1)

[50]
Total: [100]

GROUP DYNAMICS

This module covers the following aspects of personnel management:

Unit 3.1
Group development and structure

Unit 3.2
Group effectiveness

Unit 3.3
Group cohesion

Unit 3.5
Cooperation and competition

Unit 3.4
Influence in groups

Learning objectives

When you have completed this module, you should be able to do the following:

- Explain what a group is.
- Differentiate between formal and informal groups in the workplace.
- Explain group formation from perspectives such as groups based on organisational structure, workflow and human needs.
- Describe group structure, referring to roles and relationships among the members and the forces that maintain the group's organisation such as leadership and group norms.
- Explain what groups do for their members to satisfy personal needs.
- Explain what groups do for an enterprise to contribute to its success.
- Discuss the factors which influence group behaviour and performance.
- Discuss the advantages and disadvantages of group decisions and performance and how this can be improved.
- Explain what is meant by group cohesiveness, how it develops and how it influences group effectiveness.
- Discuss the factors which influence group cohesion such as success, group size, stable membership and external threats.
- Explain group influence by referring to conformity and social facilitation.
- Explain group conflict, referring to causes and consequences.
- Explain the managerial approach to group conflict.
- Discuss the effects of cooperation and competition.

Key terms

group	formal group	informal group
interacting groups	co-acting groups	counter-acting groups
reference groups	social groups	interest groups
conformity	social facilitation	

Starting point

Recent studies have found surprising reasons why some companies are more successful than others.

Employers these days know that it is important to understand how individuals work and to find ways to help them develop. However, especially in the multifaceted world of international trade and industry, there is another noticeable trend in the workplace: more and more of the work that is done is done by people working in teams. A recent study, published in *The Harvard Business Review*, found that in the past twenty years 'the time spent by managers and employees in collaborative activities has ballooned by 50 per cent or more'. The study found that, in a number of enterprises, many employees spent over seventy-five per cent of their time interacting with their co-workers.

Since the realisation that teams of people come up with new ideas more quickly than individuals working alone, managers in Silicon Valley have expressed a preference for their software engineers to work in groups. People working in groups also recognise the flaws of their software more easily and solve problems more effectively. In addition, research has found individuals who work as part of a team generally attain higher standards of work and experience greater levels of job satisfaction. A research survey conducted in 2015 revealed that employers perceived higher levels of profitability when workers collaborated more within teams. Nowadays, teamwork is the dominant work model in commercial and international enterprises as well as in civil service and educational institutions.

To rise above the competition, employers should focus not just on individual performance and output, but on how they can reap the benefits of individuals working together as part of teams.

Everyone belongs to a variety of groups which are part of your daily life, such as family, school, college, sport and the community you live in, friendship and as South Africans.

One needs to ask oneself the following questions: What is a group? How are they formed? Why do they exist? What makes a group successful? How does a group function in the workplace? How do we deal with conflict in a group or between different groups? What is the effect of cooperation and competition in a group? All of these questions will be discussed in this module.

Figure 3.1 We are all part of a group.

UNIT 3.1 Group development and structure

Most people spend the better part of their time at work working within a group environment rather than as individuals. One of management's top priorities and functions in any organisation is to group individuals in order to perform a specific task.

3.1.1 What is a group?

Definition
A **group** can be defined as two or more individuals interacting with each other to achieve a particular goal, or who share a collective identity and have universal norms.

Characteristics of a group
A group consists of many individuals who:
- have a mutual goal or objective to be achieved to which they all agreed to
- are aware of one another's skills and abilities to achieve the group's goals
- are consciously interacting with one another to achieve this goal or objective
- relate to one another
- have negotiating skills to confront and reconcile differences
- are interdependent of one another
- agree that he or she belongs to the group
- have mutual trust among members
- have effective leadership to motivate a group through difficult situations
- get support in terms of training, resources needed, and performance evaluations
- are committed to helping their group succeed.

Figure 3.2 A group of people

> **DEFINITION**
>
> **group** – two or more individuals interacting with each other to achieve a particular goal or meet specific needs

Women are one of the fastest growing groups of car consumers

Did you know that women influence 85% of car buying decisions? And that women are one of the fastest growing groups of car consumers in the world? Just this year, we saw Saudi Arabian women finally being allowed to obtain driver's licences.

So, what are women looking for in a car? According to a survey conducted by Kelley Blue Book, women are likely to prefer non-luxury sedans and SUVs with safety ranking higher on the priority list than durability and reliability.

Factors to consider:

- The survey highlights that women prioritise value and practicality and that a woman's rational needs seem to be important
- Stephanie Teixeira, Marketing Manager at car retailer, getWorth, says that other research suggests that only 38% of woman are confident about buying a car, and generally take 75 days to make a car purchase.

Although the car industry is no longer a man's world, research shows that women are still apprehensive when it comes to the car-buying process.

According to a study done by CDK Global, women used the words 'stressed,' 'overwhelmed,' 'taken advantage of' and 'panic' when reviewing their in-dealership experience. It appears that many women still feel patronised or fear when it comes to buying a car. Kelley Blue Book shares five tips for women buying a car.

1. Do your research
You cannot do enough research when it comes to buying the car of your dreams. Go online and do your homework to ensure it ticks all the boxes both practically and aesthetically. Find out how much the car sells for and whether there are different options or models available. The more you know, the better equipped you are when it comes to the actual buying process.

2. Stay in control of your outcomes
Once you are armed with all the information you could have obtained, contact your chosen dealership or online car-buying site.

If a salesperson is pushy, disrespectful or intimidating, do not do business with them. You decide the course of your car-buying experience. Be upfront and remember, you are the one in control.

3. Test drive before buying
Take the car of your choice for a test drive. If you have a few cars on your list, test drive all of them and pick the one that you enjoy driving the most. Do not let a salesperson persuade you to choose something else.

4. Don't just sign on the dotted line
Take your time. Make sure you read and understand the contracts given to you and don't be afraid to ask for a more precise explanation if you are unsure of something. Do not sign agreements to 'just get it over and done with'.

5. Buy a car online
Decide whether you want to buy privately, through a dealership or online. If you choose to go through a dealership, do your homework on the dealership options around you.

If it is through a website, be sure to check the credentials and read the online reviews. If you want to buy privately, always take someone with you, not only for safety reasons but also to assist you in the inspection of the car.

CDK stats show that purchasing a car online is proving more and more popular with women.

In the last six months alone, getWorth has seen a 6.63% increase in the ratio of female to male visitors as well as a 20% increase in overall female visitors to the site.

Wheels24's Janine Van der Post is an avid petrolhead and shares her thoughts on what she looks for in cars, "Stylish designs, impressive power figures to match and dynamics have always been key points. At the same time, I have always loved SUVs and bakkies just as much. Now as a mother and a wife, my requirements are still the same but perhaps in a different order."

"With a little person to consider, as well as the safety of my husband, my priorities have shifted. While good looks are still important, a large boot is vital, just as much as having numerous storage compartments throughout a car. I love seat pockets behind the front row, just as much as Isofix and safety features are now essentials."

"But just because I'm driving a mommy-van or a SUV, doesn't mean I don't want the kind of power and torque figures which will leave me lagging or unable to pull a quick overtake when necessary."

Read the article above and answer the following questions.

1   The author of this article refers to women as a group. Do you agree? Explain your answer.
2   This study can be useful for specific departments in an organisation. Name two departments in an organisation that will benefit from this study. Give a reason for your answer.
3   What do think are the differences between men and women buying cars?

When you started as N4-students at the college, you were all individuals, not yet a group. As soon as you started to interact with each other, you became a group, a class.

Today, we are all familiar with WhatsApp-groups. Most families and friends form their own WhatsApp-groups. People who want to organise an event form a WhatsApp-group; students working on a project form a WhatsApp-groups, etc.

Why do we all form these WhatsApp-groups? We all have either the same goal, objective or want to interact or communicate with one another.

Figure 3.3 WhatsApp icon

3.1.2 Formal versus informal groups in the workplace

The formation of groups is usually a natural process. Groups are either created by management to accomplish the goals of the organisation (formal) or by the employees themselves to satisfy their own social needs (informal).

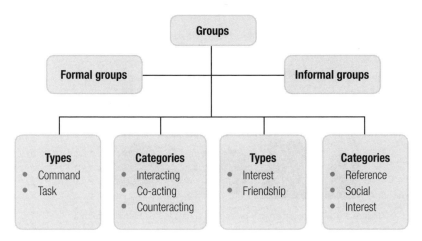

Figure 3.4 The various types and categories of groups

Formal groups in the workplace

An organisation deliberately develops **formal groups**. The group's goals and activities are directly related to the achievement of the organisational goals, which are based on the structure of the organisation that may comprise departments, sections, committees, etc.

Table 3.1 Characteristics of formal groups

Formal groups	
Structure	Pre-determined/planned
Goal	Profit – the organisational goal
Authority and responsibilities	Defined by management through the establishment of • line of command • authority
Nature	Formed for a specific purpose, temporary or permanent
Behaviour of members	Formal, according to rules and regulations of the organisation
Communication	Formal channels, systematic
Supervision	Easy
Superiors	Pressure from superiors

Types of formal groups

Command groups

Command groups consist of superiors and subordinates. This type of group is responsible for completing a specific task. For example, the marketing manager is working with a group of sales representatives.

Figure 3.5 Marketing manager presenting figures to sales representatives

Task groups

Task groups are a group of individuals who are formed to complete a specific task assigned to them. Once they accomplish the task, they return to their groups of origin. These groups formed because the members have specialised skills and they are allowed to go beyond the hierarchical lines of authority. For example, labour unions, such as COSATU, NEHAWU and SACTWU.

Categories of formal groups
Formal groups can be categorised according to the way they interact.

Interacting groups
The work (output) of one group is the input for another group, for example in an automotive production line by moving the parts, or semi-finished products, from station to station until it is a finished product.

Co-acting groups
The work done by different groups in an organisation is dependent on that of other groups. They work at the same time.

Counteracting groups
These groups work on opposing sides but work together to solve their differences. For example, management and trade unions do collective bargaining to solve wage issues.

Informal groups in the workplace
Employees of an organisation form **informal groups**. These employees share the same interests, feelings, attitudes and/or social needs. An informal group does not necessarily share the same goal as that of the organisation.

DEFINITION

formal group – a group deliberately developed by managers to achieve organisational goals

---

Table 3.2 Characteristics of informal groups

Informal group	
Structure	Spontaneously
Goal	Satisfaction of own personal needs
Authority and responsibilities	Authority is linked to a person, not a position
Nature	Permanent, individual decides when to leave the group
Behaviour of members	Informal, according to the individual's or group's interest
Communication	Informal communication, according to the relationship within the group (grapevine)
Supervision	Difficult
Superiors	No pressure from superiors

Types of informal groups

Interest groups

These groups form spontaneously and are not related to the organisation they work for. Members join this group to achieve a common objective like sport or culture.

Friendship groups

Employees form friendship groups outside the work environment. Members form social ties and are attached because they are of similar age, share the same tradition or even support the same sports team.

Figure 3.6 An informal group of friends

> **DEFINITION**
>
> **informal group** – a group formed by employees of an organisation to achieve their own goals or to meet their own needs

Categories of informal groups

Informal groups can also be categorised according to the way they interact.

Reference groups

Members of a reference group share the same beliefs, values, preferences and attitudes. For example, they are attending the same church (the same religion).

Social groups

Members of a social group have a shared sense of belonging. They can identify with one another. Members also influence each other's behaviour and personality. For example, friends and family.

Interest groups

Although this is an informal group, the members are formally organised. They share the same concerns, problems or issues and want to find a solution that would benefit everyone in the group. For example, an environmental group campaigning against a new development out of concern for the fauna and flora.

Power Break 3.2   GROUP WORK

Read the following statements and in each case indicate if it is an example of a formal or informal group. Write 'formal' or 'informal' next to the number and give a reason for your answer.

1	People who organise a carpool to get to work every day.
2	Individuals who are united by their common interest.
3	The behaviour of the people is regulated by the rules and regulations framed with an intention to attain rationality and efficiency.
4	Authority in these groups is earned or given permissively by the members of the group.
5	Groups are quite large because personal relations are of no concern.
6	Groups that are not controlled by the organisation.
7	Authority in these groups is acquired through delegation from the top downwards.
8	Groups can be abolished at the discretion of the proper authority.
9	These groups have a well-planned strategy for fighting with the management about their grievances.
10	The manager decides about the activities of each individual and his or her interaction with others.

3.1.3 Group formation from different perspectives

The formation of groups can be classified in terms of the group's organisational structure, workflow and human needs.

Groups based on organisational structure

The formal group within the organisation has a specific reason for existence or goal they want to achieve. The needs of the organisation justify their existence. The group consists of a manager and many subordinates. For example, a production department is a formal group with a production manager, assistant manager, supervisors and general employees.

> **Flashback to N4**: In *Succeed in Personnel Management N4*, Module 2, we studied the different organisational structures, line structure, line and staff structure, geographical structure, etc. Refer back to Module 2 to remind yourself of the different structures.

Groups based on workflow

These groups form as a result of the interaction between workers throughout the organisation. These are informal groups. The members are mutually dependent on each other, and their work is related. This helps them to speed up and improve communication and ultimately to complete a task or tasks. These groups are not recognised by the organisation but are justified because they improve the workflow and because the members find it more satisfying than formal groups. Consider, for example, a production organisation's workflow: the cost accountant does the production planning; the engineer can then design the systems and processes; now the actual manufacturing and assembly take place; and the quality manager inspects the products to make sure there are no defects.

Groups based on human needs

Groups are primarily developed to satisfy the social needs of people such as giving and receiving affection, association with others and general acceptance. The members receive constant feedback about their behaviour which satisfies higher-order needs. Management should link the group's goal with that of the organisation. This will create maximum long-term organisational effectiveness and the satisfaction of each individual's need(s) as well.

3.1.4 Group structure

Every group that exists has a specific structure. This structure will affect the performance of the group and also create an environment of order. The group's roles, interaction, leadership and norms are some of the structural variables that we will discuss in the next few paragraphs. These roles, interaction, leadership and norms develop over time and determine the success of a group.

Exam tip: Do not get confused between organisational and group structures.

Group roles

A role is the member's part to play in a particular situation. It is a set of behavioural patterns and associated attitudes related to someone in a specific position in a group. These patterns and attitudes will be stipulated and will have to be consistent. For example, the sales director in an organisation is crucial in improving the organisation's revenue and sales, to organise and monitor the department's general performance and to support the sales staff. The sales representative's roles are to promote and sell products and services, to reach out to the customers and to achieve the agreed upon sales targets.

Group interaction

The interaction between members of a group can be either positive or negative. The positive side is that it leads to a friendship which will lead to greater cooperation and improved performances. On the negative side, it can lead to conflict between individuals. This will be counterproductive and ultimately damaging to the performance of the group.

Group leadership

Each group has a leader at any given time. Leadership is one of the most important keys to the group's success. The leader is someone who has the ability and skills to inspire and motivate the members of the group to perform to the best of their abilities and to reach the group and organisation's goals. The person formally appointed is not necessarily the leader. In Module 4 we will deal with leadership in detail.

Group norms

The interaction within a group over time leads to the development of group norms. Norms define the generally accepted standard behaviour of the member of the group. Norms provide the group with boundaries of behaviour within which group members can act. Norms also help the members of the group to establish a common direction and thus strengthen the group's culture. Members obeying this standard behaviour can determine the success and continued existence or failure and separation of the group.

Norms can be formal or informal. For example, a formal norm is for a student to attend compulsory classes. When he or she does not attend, he or she will not be granted admission to the examination. This is a direct result of not obeying the enforced norm. Informal norms are based on the general interaction between members of the group. An example of a group norm is not making up false and disrespectful stories about one another.

Group status

Group status specifies the importance of each member of the group, and refers to the specific position of the individual.

Group size

The size of the group affects the general manner in which the group behaves. Smaller groups tend to work and complete tasks faster. However, larger groups might be more proficient in solving a problem.

Figure 3.7 The group structure will depend on the group function.

Power Break 3.3 INDIVIDUAL WORK

Answer the following questions.

1 What is a group structure?
2 All work groups have a structure that dictates the behaviour of its members and makes the reaching of a group's goals possible. Various factors influence the structure of the group.
   Name and explain the factors that influence the structure of a group.
3 Indicate if the following statements are TRUE or FALSE. Write only 'true' or 'false' next to the question number.
   3.1 Formal groups help to solve problems.
   3.2 Group norms refer to group diversity.
   3.3 Groups in an organisation can make a positive or a negative contribution to the organisational success.

UNIT 3.2 Group effectiveness

3.2.1 What groups do to satisfy the personal needs of their members

The following describes the personal needs of individuals working in groups:

- Individuals need to have a clear understanding of the aims and goals of the group to which they have mutually agreed. They need to know what they are accountable for producing, and what the rewards, recognition and compensation are to empower them within the group.
- Individuals need to feel that they are treated with respect. This way they will respond with respect to their group members and leaders, and they will respond with responsible actions. In a respectful workplace, everyone is equal; he or she has different jobs and roles.
- Individuals need to feel part of the group. They, therefore, need to know there are good guidelines and procedures in place, and that they have access to information as quickly as anyone else in the workplace.
- Individuals need to bring their viewpoints and knowledge to the group; there needs to be effective communication within the group as well as with the organisation.
- In case of conflict, individuals need to express themselves openly and honestly for the group to handle conflict in a constructive way.
- Individuals need to be involved in decision-making relevant to their jobs. They need to be involved and feel empowered. This will improve their performances and make them willing to work through difficult situations.
- Individuals need to trust the leader and want to be happy with the way they are led. They want a sense of being on the right track, going somewhere that is defined and important. Individuals like to know that someone who is trustworthy is in charge.
- Individuals need to feel confident that they have a product that can be successful and a company that understands and listens to the marketplace.
- Individuals expect timely and accurate payment of wages, adequate training, safe working conditions, a full explanation of all company policies and especially of their job responsibilities, and fair and constructive feedback from their supervisor.
- Individuals need a work environment free from discrimination, harassment and unsafe conditions.
- Individuals also need job satisfaction, employee recognition, financial benefits and job stability.

As an individual at work, you need to feel you are a productive member of a group that is accomplishing something together. Once the characteristics above are evident in a group, group work will flourish.

There are many models for effective groups. In 1965, the psychologist, Bruce Tuckman, proposed that there are five stages of group development: forming, storming, norming, performing and adjourning. This will be discussed in Unit 3.3 Group cohesion.

3.2.2 What groups do for an organisation to contribute to its success

Every member of a group has a role to play to ensure they operate effectively and to reach their objective or goal. The role of the member might not always be the same; members may adopt different roles at different times during the group's existence.

- Problem-solving. A group will solve a problem much easier when the members go through a process of sharing their thoughts, discussions, actions and decisions. The problem-solving process will help the group to find creative and diverse solutions for their problem. The work-load is also shared by the members of the group, and as a result, the members will experience less stress.
- Behaviour standards. The group will set standards and guidelines to direct the behaviour of members. The members' actions, attitudes, values and norms are set to retain their membership. The standard of behaviour influences the group positively, and also the organisation as a whole.
- Goal-achievement. Groups will be more effective when they work towards a specific goal. We have members work together to reach a goal because we know that together we can achieve more than we can separately.
- Leadership development. Informal leaders will surface from groups. The potential of future leaders in the organisation will develop.

3.2.3 Factors which influence group behaviour and performance

Factors such as leadership, cohesion, group norms, individual roles and the nature of the tasks can have an impact on the behaviour and performance of a group.

- Leadership. A group needs the correct direction, instructions and guidance to perform at its best. Good leadership will motivate the group to help achieve the group's objectives.
- Cohesiveness. Group cohesiveness allows group members to work together and to feel positive about the task at hand. Group members need to be able to freely interact and cooperate with one another. Group members who work together as a unit work more effectively. Any negative feeling may have alarming results.
- Member motivation. A group will be better motivated if all members are involved in setting the group's goals and where all members are working together to accomplish these goals. A group will perform even better with more motivation if the members have a pleasant workplace, if there is room to grow, if they get positive feedback and if management is supportive and transparent. Everyone will do his or her part to achieve the goals of the group.
- Group norms. Each group has its own set of unspoken rules that control the way an individual behaves in a group. These norms are the issues important to the group. Without group norms, individuals would have no understanding of how to act in certain situations.

- Individual roles. In a group where each member performs a specific job or task to help the group to accomplish a group task, the performance of the group will be increased.
- Environment. In the workplace, it is often assumed that employees who are more satisfied with the physical environment are more likely to produce better work outcomes.
- Tasks. There are different types of tasks given to a group: In **additive** tasks, the group's performance depends on the sum of everybody's effort. In **conjunctive** tasks, the effort of every group member is important to work towards the goal, even the least skilled member. In **disjunctive** tasks, an individual finds the solution.

Figure 3.8 People working in a busy but organised environment

3.2.4 Advantages and disadvantages of group decisions and performance

A group often needs to make a decision or decisions. Members will collaborate and then choose the alternative available to them. Variation can be seen as a useful tool for the organisation. Let us compare the advantages and disadvantages of group decision-making.

Advantages of group decisions and performance

- More information. The more informed group members are, the better decision the group makes. A group is much more equipped and informed than an individual.
- A diversity of views. Every member has their view of a specific issue, problem or topic. The members' different views will be an advantage because there will be a variation of

DEFINITIONS

additive – all group members perform the same task to improve the bigger task

conjunctive – every group member has a different task to do fo'r the group to complete a task

disjunctive – a group task is completed when a single solution or decision of an individual is adopted by the group

views. This is also the reason why there are varied approaches to solving a problem. As group decisions tend to cover a greater area, they provide better insight into decision-making.

- Greater acceptability. The view and decision of a group have more credibility than that of an individual member because there was a greater consensus.
- Expert opinions. There may be some group decisions that require an expert opinion. The group can either include experts or call them from outside to form a separate group to decide on a particular issue.
- A degree of involvement. As soon as members are involved in the decision-making, it will strengthen the group and minimise the amount of resistance and friction among members.
- Communication. Group decision-making promotes discussion and communication in the organisation.

Disadvantages of group decisions and performance

- Time-consuming. Getting the members organised or to coordinate a meeting and to arrive at a consensus can be a long process.
- Individual domination. Very often one member might dominate and try to influence others when a group needs to make a decision. Other members fade away, thereby defeating the very purpose of group discussion.
- Pressure. The pressure on the group to reach a solution or consensus might lead to popular rather than effective decisions. It can also result in a compromise. The solution offered is not essentially the best. It is, instead, a compromise acceptable as a mid-point to all concerned.
- Expensive. A group's decision-making process is quite expensive in terms of time, money, energy and working hours.
- Sub-groups. The formation of groups into sub-groups can influence group decision-making.

How to improve group decisions and performance

- Know your team.
- Set appropriate goals.
- Define roles and responsibilities.
- People will work harder in groups when they feel that they are contributing to the group and that their work is visible to and valued by the other group members.
- Providing rewards for performance may increase the effort of the individual group members. (If the rewards are not perceived as equitable, they may also lead to upward social comparison and a reduction in effort by other members.)
- Tackle problems quickly with good feedback.
- Break down barriers.
- Focus on communication and adequate information sharing.
- Pay attention.

The Griffiths Commission

The President established a task force, the Griffiths Commission, to investigate the Winterberg aviation disaster. The chairman was Mr Griffiths. One of the people in the task force was William Rodgers, who initially wanted to refuse to join because of his dislike of working in groups.

Despite his misgivings, he did accept the appointment because he realised the importance of investigating what had caused the disaster – one of the biggest in South African aviation history.

The 12-member group was given the following brief:

1. Determine the circumstances surrounding the disaster and investigate possible causes.
2. Make recommendations for actions that should be taken to avoid a similar thing happening again.

At the first meeting of the task force, it was decided that the investigation should be completed within 120 days. However, no detailed plan was put in place for how to run the investigation. This was of great concern to Rodgers. It was only when the group met for the third time that they really understood what they had to do. The chairman of the commission said that in order to keep strict control on the investigation, no one in the group should have access to information that any of the others did not have access to at the same time. For this reason, all 12 members of the team flew together to the scene where the disaster happened.

Rodgers did not agree with running the investigation in this way. In his view, he thought he would be able to contribute more to the investigation if he worked individually. However, the chairman of the commission was firm that Rodgers needed to work as part of the group.

The group held a number of closed meetings to discuss their findings. After every closed meeting, they held a public meeting in the interest of openness and transparency, and to prevent the perception that any findings against SAA would be covered up.

After one month of combined group meetings, four subgroups were formed, each to look into a different aspect of the disaster. It did not take Rodgers long to write a report of his findings, which he presented to the chairman of the commission. The commission, however, did not share the report with the other group members, as he wanted to avoid it having an effect on the other members' findings.

All group members were involved in compiling the final report, with each one writing a section of the report, which the other groups edited. Rodgers found the lack of discussion in this process exasperating, especially at the final meeting at which time the commission made its recommendations.

Nine recommendations were put forward, and all nine were accepted for inclusion as part of the report with very few amendments. Rodgers proposed an additional recommendation. After much resistance and dispute, this was included in an amended form.

The final Griffiths Report did put forward a reasonable account of the likely causes of the disaster. In addition, it included a list of recommendations. Dissatisfied with the process, Rodgers wrote his own report. Mercifully, since the Winterberg disaster, there has been no similar incident.

Source: *General Management*, J. Kroon (Ed), 1990. Reprinted by permission of Pearson Business.

Read the article above and answer the following questions.

1. Was the Griffiths Commission a formal or informal group? Why?
2. Did the commission meet the requirements for an effective group? Give reasons for your answer.

UNIT 3.3 **Group cohesion**

3.3.1 An introduction to group cohesion

Group cohesion is an essential contributor to the overall success of a group and the organisation as a whole.

What is meant by group cohesion?

Cohesion is a process of sticking together and forming a united whole while following the group's goals and objectives. When the members of the whole group fit together well, they are cohesive, for example, a cohesive family whose members join in and help one another, from making dinner to painting the house. Members of cohesive groups work together more efficiently and feel more positive about their work, and they have bonds that link them to one another and the group as a whole.

Development of group cohesion

A cohesive group usually has the following characteristics:
* Members have the same goals/objectives.
* Members have the same skills and abilities.
* Members have the same needs and come from the same background.
* Members have the same interests.
* Groups tend to be small.
* Members interact with one another.
* Members are from the same age group.
* Group members stick together whether they experience great success or failure.
* Members are incredibly loyal to one another.

Group cohesion develops over time. Tuckman's five-stage model of group development consists of the following stages.

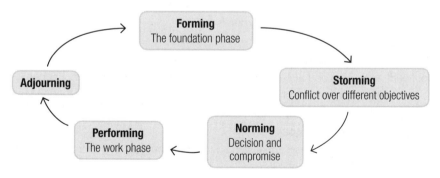

Figure 3.9 The five-stage model of Bruce Tuckman

> **DEFINITION**
>
> **cohesion** – a process of sticking together and forming a united whole while following the group's goals and objectives

Forming

- Forming is the first stage of development of a group. This stage is very similar to your orientation day at college or your first day at your new job. Members of the team introduce themselves to one another and are at this stage very friendly and civil to each other. There is a feeling of excitement for the start of something new.
- There is still uncertainty about the leadership, the skills of the members, ground rules, specific rules and the project's goals. As time passes and the members get to familiarise themselves; roles and responsibilities will begin to form. At this stage, members focus more on the people than the work itself. The group is not yet very productive.
- As soon as the members think of themselves as a group, they enter the storming phase.

Storming

- During this stage, the members become more and more aware of the other members' characteristics. These unique characteristics may annoy and frustrate you. This is very similar to you being in a relationship. When you are in love, you think your partner is perfect, with no faults. As you get to know the person better over time, you see there are definite flaws. In the storming-stage, just like in a relationship, you have to decide if you are willing to embrace the flaws or if you will end the relationship.
- In this stage, members of the group also realise the demands of the work and feel the tension to complete the task. The initial feelings of excitement and being civil with other members in the forming-stage are now replaced by the burden of the task at hand and members experiencing conflict. This is also the stage where members will test each other and try to determine a hierarchy of leadership. Once the group puts the hierarchy in place, they will move on to the next stage, norming.

Norming

- In this stage, members develop close relationships with one another. Members also start to notice and appreciate the strengths, contributions and efforts of their fellow members. The group is now highly cohesive and experience a sense of comradeship. The group moves to the next stage as soon as the group structure is solid and the norms (expected behaviour) of the group is set.

Performing

- Stage 4 is one step closer to success. During this stage, the members are very confident, motivated and at ease with the project and will operate without supervision. Each member knows precisely what to do and what is expected of him or her. The group's structure or hierarchy is not a source of conflict anymore, but instead a mechanism to reach their goal.
- For permanent groups, this is the final stage, but for temporary groups, there is an additional stage, called adjourning.

Adjourning

- Once the task is completed, the project is completed, or once the group reached their goal, the group separates. This phase is sometimes known as mourning. The group's performance is no longer a priority. Members have grown close to each other. The members' feelings can range from excitement because of the completion of a successful task to sadness as all the members go their separate way.

Power Break 3.5 INDIVIDUAL WORK

Identify the stage of the group-development process in each of the following situations.

 **1** Close relationship	
 **2** Say goodbye	
 **3** Orientation day	
 **4** Frustrated	
 **5** Group hierarchy	

Influence of group cohesion on group effectiveness

There is a direct link between the group's cohesion and productivity, effectiveness and efficiency of the organisation's output. This can be seen as advantages and explained as follows:

- Members of a highly cohesive group generally experience less work-related stress and promote high morale.
- It leads to lower staff turnover and less absenteeism. Group members do not want to disappoint their fellow members by being absent, which will result in a member or members needing to do extra work or work more extended hours.
- Cohesive groups with similar status, attitudes and cultural background experience a high degree of job satisfaction.
- Cohesive groups result in higher production and better cooperation.
- Cohesive groups are generally more creative and more energetic.

Power Break 3.6   INDIVIDUAL WORK

Reread the case study, 'The Griffiths Commission' (Power Break 3.4), and answer the following questions by using examples from the case study.

1   Use the given phases of group development and identify the commission's phases of development.
2   Did the group have cohesion? Motivate your answer.

In a workplace, it is not always possible to choose which group you are in and therefore you have to adapt to the group you are in. You might naturally work better with some members of the group than others. Let us discuss factors that affect the cohesiveness of a group.

3.3.2 Factors affecting the group cohesiveness

The following factors influence group cohesion.

- The group's success. The more successful the group, the more cohesive they become. Success has a positive effect on groups. Everyone enjoys success and the more successful you are, the more motivated you will be to repeat the success or even to be more successful.
- The size of the group. Smaller groups (seven or fewer members) are generally more cohesive than larger groups (more than seven members). Group interaction and communication become problematic with more than 10–12 members (larger groups) in a group. Each member gets less opportunity to interact with one another. Members also tend to put in less effort, because they believe someone else in the group will make up for their slack. In smaller groups there is no place to hide; everyone has to participate, communicate and put in the effort.
- The work environment. If the work environment promotes and facilitates communication and interaction between members, the groups will be highly cohesive. Factors such as noise, the type of work or the layout of the work environment may have a negative effect on group cohesion.

- The management style. The group leadership style influences the relationship between the members of the group, and the relationship between the group and the organisation. The leader should give guidance, encouragement and also provide opportunities for group participation and to resolve conflict effectively.
- Group status. Group status is linked to the group's success. Successful groups are often rewarded or mentioned and/or congratulated by management in emails and/or newsletters. Group members enjoy the higher status, which creates more cohesive groups. Outsiders will want to become part of this success and status while existing members will work hard to 'defend' their place in the group.
- Inter- and intra-group competition. Intergroup competition is between various groups in an organisation. Intra-group competition is between members of a specific group. Competition between members can have a positive (every member improves their performance) or negative (conflict) effect on cohesiveness.
- Group goals. Individuals join a group because the group's goals coincide with their own and with that the group can help them achieve their personal goals too.
- Lasting relationships. Like in any relationship, people who remain in the same group for a long period are more attracted to one another. Members get to know each other well over time and build solid relationships. They know each other's strengths and weaknesses. Therefore, groups should not be broken up unnecessarily.
- External threats. When the group faces a common external threat, members will work together in solidarity to 'defend' the group.

Figure 3.10 Factors affecting the group cohesiveness

Figure 3.11 Smaller groups of between five and seven members generally work better.

Power Break 3.7 INDIVIDUAL WORK

Choose a factor from Column B that matches the description in Column A. Write only the letter (a–i) next to the question number (1–9).

	COLUMN A		COLUMN B
1	Leadership style influences the relationship between the members of the group.	a)	Lasting relationships
2	Successful groups are often rewarded or mentioned and/or congratulated by management in emails and/or newsletters.	b)	External threats
3	Communication becomes problematic with more than 10–12 members.	c)	The group's success
4	Members will work together in solidarity to 'defend' the group.	d)	Group goals
5	They know each other's strengths and weaknesses.	e)	Inter- and intra-group competition
6	Success has a positive effect on the groups.	f)	The group's status
7	Factors such as the type of work may have a negative effect on group cohesion.	g)	The work environment
8	Competition between members can have a positive or negative effect on cohesiveness.	h)	Size of the group
9	The group wants to achieve the same things than you as an individual.	i)	Management style

UNIT 3.4 **Influence in groups**

3.4.1 Role of groups in the workplace

- In groups, each group member is involved. Everyone's strengths and skill levels are best utilised.
- Information is shared between team members, and communication between the group and the entire organisation is effective.
- A group can produce a wide range of possible solutions for each specific problem and then determine the most effective solution through collective input and interaction.
- Teamwork gives people common goals to pursue. It encourages individuals to encourage other members of the team and to help achieve the common goals.
- A team often provides more accurate, innovative and practical solutions to problems than individuals.
- Teamwork usually yields better final results, and individuals show better within a group.
- Workers are more emotionally positive and are better off sharing knowledge, learning and taking on responsibilities when they experience the personal safety of being part of an effective team.
- There is a good chance that individuals will take risks when they experience the safety of being part of an effective team, as they receive support and assurance of participation in a group. It makes more creative and innovative solutions possible.
- By using teamwork, an organisation's decision-making process can be understood much better by its members.
- A group can sometimes handle complicated, confusing, in-depth and relevant problems more effectively than individuals can. This is because the variety of skills and experience can be better suited to severe problems.
- Groups can complete tasks and solve problems faster than individuals through the effective allocation of human resources and the creation of various ideas in a short period.
- New ideas and measures can be implemented more efficiently through effective collaboration with the entire organisation if employees have a sense of involvement.
- Innovation and creativity can be improved by the more significant and greater inputs that come from team involvement.
- Effective teamwork is fun for the people concerned, and it can enhance motivation and morale for the entire organisation.

3.4.2 Group influence on the individual

In some organisations, individuals work independently and perform their task, but in many cases, employees work in a group, and they have to interact with other members. It is important to understand how being in a group can affect the performance of the task. We will explain the group's influence on the individual by referring to the following:

- Conformity
- Social facilitation

Conformity

Conformity in the workplace refers to the behaviour or actions that follow the accepted rules of the workplace. For example, a dress code. Even though plain casual clothes have replaced the traditional office clothes, some businesses, e.g. banks and law offices, still have conservative dress code policies in place for employees to adhere to.

This means that the individual will tend to change his or her belief or behaviour, so they can fit in with the group. This involves the social influence on the individual to change. Some refer to conformity as yielding (giving in) to the pressure of the group. This means the group determines the 'normal' and the individual gives in to this 'normal'.

Examples of conformity occur in almost every industry and every aspect of employment. Some important types of conformity include the following:

- Compliance. The individual changes his or her behaviour while privately disagreeing with the group, e.g. to say you like classical music because many people in the group like classical music, but you do not like this kind of music.
- Identification. This occurs when people conform to what is expected of them but only while they are in the group. This also occurs when a person does not have the knowledge and looks to the group for information and direction.
- Internalisation. This occurs when we change our behaviour because we want to be like another person. This is more permanent, e.g. where two people from different cultural groups get involved, and the one accepts the other's culture and makes this culture part of his or her life.

Figure 3.12 The individual wants to fit in.

> **DEFINITION**
>
> **conformity** – the behaviour or actions that follow the accepted rules of the workplace

Social facilitation

Some researchers refer to social facilitation as the audience effect. This is when a member changes his or her behaviour as soon as he or she is in the presence of others (the group). You might recognise this behaviour in yourself or some of your friends.

The presence of others can have a positive or a negative effect on the individual's behaviour.

Some members feel a degree of anxiety when they are in the presence of others. They feel that their behaviour is always being assessed and are uncertain if they performed well enough. Other individuals get distracted by others. Some are so focused on the others and to please them that they neglect their own performance.

On the positive side, some members tend to perform much better when they are watched or competing with others doing the same task. Certain other members perform better with just the idea of someone else in their presence. They are more thorough and less prone to make mistakes.

For example, when one employee is busy with a task, he or she does it with little enthusiasm. The work is difficult and time-consuming. As soon as he or she does the same work in a group, he or she will be more positive and energetic. The performance is better because everyone else is working hard with you and you do not want to be the one not performing.

The opposite example can also apply. When you are a self-motivated individual, you can work and perform well on your own. As soon as you work in a group, you feel intimidated by other's performances and doubt yourself and perform below your usual standard.

Power Break 3.8   CASE STUDY

We can all relate to one or more of these ten things about social psychology mentioned in the article. Read the article below and answer the following questions.

Ten things you should know about how people behave in groups

Social psychology research has made several fascinating findings about the behaviour of people in a group situation, often revealing things that might surprise you. Ten key findings are:

1. People may act quite differently when there are many people present. In what is known as the bystander effect, in an incident such as an accident, when there are many people present, the likelihood of an individual stepping forward to help decreases.

2. People will try very hard to do what an authority figure tells them to. To obey an authority figure, people may go to extremes, often even behaving recklessly.

3. People feel the need to fit in, which makes them follow group behaviour. The majority of people will follow the pack and go along with group behaviour, even if they think what they are doing is not right.

4. How we behave in a social situation can change according to the context.

Our social behaviour can be strongly influenced by the situation in which we find ourselves. In a psychology experiment carried out in a prison, participants were given various roles, such as correctional officers and prisoners. The participants showed extreme reactions, taking on the roles they were given in such a way that those placed in a position of power started abusing their power, while those in the role of prisoners showed signs of severe anxiety and stress.

5. People lean towards information that is in line with the way they already see the world.

In behaviour that is known as expectation confirmation, people tend to believe information that is similar to what they already think is true, and they tend to disregard any information that does not match what they already believe.

6. To help us understand what is happening around us, we often categorise people as members of particular groups. This can make us perceive people in stereotypical ways.

When we think about people as belonging to certain groups, we have a tendency to focus on the differences between the groups, and to think that people within the same group are more similar. As a result, stereotypes and prejudice develop.

7. Our attitude to something plays a major role in how we behave towards people.

How we feel about things may be expressed consciously or formed unconsciously, but either way these attitudes have an influence on our behaviour and approach to various social situations.

8. Our perceptions of other people and the way we expect them to behave are strongly influenced by our underlying expectations.

The way we expect people to behave is often largely based on a preconceived idea that we associate with the specific role or social group they are in. We often judge their behaviour according to the expectations that result from our inbuilt preconceptions and according to the social norms we associate with those roles.

9. We tend to blame others when things go wrong for them. However, if things do not work out for us, we don't put the blame on ourselves.

When explaining their own behaviour, people tend to associate outside factors with things that go wrong, but when they see things go wrong for others they say that they are to blame.

10. People often go with the flow, to avoid causing upset or drawing attention to themselves.

In behaviour known as groupthink, to avoid causing a scene, individuals within a group frequently go along with the crowd even if their own opinion differs from the group opinion. Groupthink often occurs when the members of the group have a lot in common. It is also common in groups that have a leader who is a very strong character, or in groups that find themselves in a stressful situation.

1 Let us discuss no. 4: The situation can also have a significant influence on social behaviour. In your groups, discuss a similar situation where you changed your behaviour because of influences.

2 Select one of the above-mentioned ten things and act out the situation. Perform it to see if the class can identify which one you have selected.

UNIT 3.5 **Cooperation and competition**

We already discussed the importance and influence of groups functioning as a unit and the effectiveness of a cohesive group, but what happens when there is conflict in a group? Let us discuss group conflict, the causes, the consequences, how managers should approach group conflict and the effects of cooperation and competition in a group.

3.5.1 Group conflict

Group conflict is an interactive problem that occurs between two or more members of a group, and as a result, the group does not perform at optimum levels. These **interdependent** members have differences of opinion that influence the interaction between them. Conflict does not necessarily mean the parties fight with each other, but because of the differences, the cooperation between them will break down. It is very important for managers to look into the reasons for group conflict and to find ways to resolve the problem.

Not all conflict situations have a negative impact or are bad for the organisation. Managers should lessen the negative impact and try to increase the positive impact. Positive conflict can inspire creative thinking, innovation and generate alternative ways to resolve problems, conflict and other challenges.

On the negative side, it may cause the parties to spend their time trying to resolve the issues surrounding the conflict, rather than the conflict itself.

Figure 3.13 Group conflict in the workplace

> **DEFINITION**
>
> **interdependent** – two or more people or groups that depend on each other

Causes of group conflict

Conflicts in the workplace could occur between individuals or groups.

In general, conflicts in the workplace may arise between individuals because of different personalities, a difference of opinion, or of a weak management style. Conflict can arise from misunderstandings, poor communication, lack of planning, frustration, stress and burnout.

We now look into more specific causes.

Win-lose situations

Very often two individuals within a group pursue the same position within the group, for example, team leader, which they cannot both concurrently achieve. Both feel very strongly that they got what it takes to be a team leader. One will get the position (win) and the other not (lose).

The method used to achieve the organisational goal

Individuals and groups may have different views on how they should go about achieving an organisational goal. This causes conflict. For example, the one member feels the organisation should invest in a greater variety of products to satisfy the needs of the customers and in return that will result in higher profits. However, the next member believes that the goal of increased profit can be achieved by cutting costs and not by investing in the production of more products.

Non-concurring status

For some people it is very important to know where they stand in relation to other people. The same thing occurs in an organisation. For example, people want to know what their relative status position in the organisation is and where they stand with regard to others. An organisation has a range of status hierarchies that change regularly.

Perceptual differences

Each person or group develop their perception of the world or their environment. Perception is based on your beliefs, values, culture, customs and traditions and this will not always be the same as those of other people. People act according to their perception of the environment.

Power Break 3.9   GROUP DISCUSSION

Read the following article about business etiquette when doing business with South Africans. This will also be applicable for groups to avoid unnecessary conflict situations.

South African business etiquette

Having good knowledge of the different cultural practices of the various South African cultural groups is vital for successful business interactions in this multicultural society. Here are some important points to remember:

- Many South Africans feel awkward about working with people they have not met. If possible, ask an existing contact who already knows the person you want to deal with to introduce you to them. If you already have South African business references, it would also be helpful to let potential business partners know about these.

- When you have your first business meeting, do not expect to discuss much business. This meeting is more of an opportunity to get to know one another and establish rapport and trust. You are much more likely to achieve a successful business relationship if you are working with someone whom you like and trust.

- Your choice of clothing is important. For men, suits and ties, with light-coloured shirts are considered appropriate. Wear a long-sleeved shirt if you are going without a jacket. For a dinner at a business associate's home, the appropriate attire is a dinner jacket. For women, dresses and skirts are considered more appropriate than pantsuits. Avoid anything that is sleeveless, too tight, or very short. In winter – the months between June and August – you need to make sure you dress warmly enough to suit the conditions.

- English is the second language of most South Africans. Therefore, it is generally accepted for business documents and written materials to be presented in English, and it is not considered necessary to translate them into an African language.

- In conversation, ensure that your tone of voice is moderate, and that you do not raise your voice. Do not interrupt someone who is speaking, as this is considered rude. Take care not to cause offence when interacting with a female associate by addressing her in a way that does not reflect her marital status. If she is married, you should not address her as 'miss', as this may be considered offensive.

- In general, South Africans tend to be very friendly and expressive of affection. Associates may shake your hand readily, but other gestures of friendship may include slapping you on the back or even holding your hand.

- When an associate shows you hospitality, such as inviting you to their home for dinner, it is appropriate to give them a small gift, such as chocolate or a bottle of wine, to show your appreciation.

- Never show disrespect to elders, whether they are involved in the business or not. In South Africa, disrespecting one's elders – whose wisdom is valued – shows very poor character. Many people would be reluctant to do business with an individual who does not show respect for elders.

- In order to prove herself in business, a woman needs to show herself to be confident in her abilities and knowledge of her subject matter, but not become aggressive should she find herself in a situation in which she feels that she is considered inferior to men.

- In certain situations, smoking may be accepted, but only after other people have finished eating. It is not considered appropriate to have conversations with servants during dinner.

- Do not point your index finger at anyone, as this is taken as rudeness. In addition, the 'V' for victory sign is considered lewd. It is also considered rude to keep your hands in your pockets while having a conversation with someone.

- When interacting with an associate, you need to be perceived as a good listener. It is important to make constant eye contact and nod your head frequently to show your agreement. It is important to appear to be a good listener.

Reread the article above. Can you think of more 'do's' and 'don'ts' that the author of this article might have missed?

Change

An organisation operates in a very dynamic environment and must be able to adapt to the changing circumstances in order to be successful. Some people and groups thrive with change; they find it exciting and see it as a challenge. Other groups, however, tend to hang on to what is familiar and known to them. They strongly resist any change and/or new developments; even more so when it is forced on them. Change creates uncertainty, which some of the groups in the organisation will resent. The difference in opinion or feelings about the change(s) – those in favour and those opposed to it – among the groups will cause conflict. Changes can be significant, such as to relocate, to install a new computer system, to merge with another organisation or they can be minor changes such as changing the members of a small team.

Interdependence

As soon as the output of one group is essential in order to allow another group to do their work, it may cause conflict. The groups are interdependent. For example, the financial manager has to wait for the other departments to submit their budgets before she can determine and complete the overall budget of the organisation.

Limited resources

An organisation has a limited amount of money and other resources. All the groups need resources to complete their tasks. Groups will compete for these resources, and each group might see their task as the most important. The more limited the resources, the more the likelihood of conflict and groups competing for the resources.

Reward structures

Other sources of conflict may arise as soon as the organisation rewards individual groups instead of all the employees for the overall performance of the organisation. All the departments in an organisation depend on each other. The sales department can only sell products if the production department produces these products. The production department can only produce the products if the finance department makes money available to buy material and to pay for the labour. When the organisation only rewards one group, for example, the sales department for increasing the sales figures, it may cause conflict.

Communication problems

Communication can be a significant cause of conflict between groups and even within a group. Examples of communication problems are semantic (language) differences, the lack of information, the grapevine, the credibility of the sender, the misinterpretation of the message, noise, etc. Groups make decisions or take action based on information received through some form of communication, which can cause problems.

Other organisational variables

Many other variables can cause problems or conflict between groups in an organisation, such as the leadership style of the managers, the type of work, the involvement of trade unions and the size of the organisation.

Power Break 3.10 INDIVIDUAL WORK

Study the following scenarios. Answer the following questions for each of the three scenarios.

1 Identify the cause of the conflict situation.
2 How would you resolve this conflict situation?

Scenario 1

For the past year, John has been employed as the sales manager of a company. It appears that his reps respond fairly well to his motivation techniques and his sales reports show good sales.

However, some reps have given negative feedback about John's management style. They complain that John gets over-involved with their sales methods and that he is quick to point out what he sees as mistakes. However, he responds quite negatively when he himself is criticised.

One of the top reps in terms of sales figures is particularly critical of John. He is threatening to resign because of the way John behaves.

Scenario 2

Ashlee and James are colleagues in the accounting department of a firm. Ashlee has worked for the company for many years, while James has worked for the company for only a few months.

The two employees each have specific tasks that they are expected to perform, and each relies on the other to complete certain jobs. While they are both proficient workers, they have very different work styles. Ashlee works consistently every day and makes sure all her tasks are done in good time. James often procrastinates, and often only finishes tasks very close to the deadline. As they often need to work together on certain jobs, Ashlee finds herself worrying about James' work as much as her own, and she feels the pressure of having to wait for James to complete something at the last minute before she can finalise her side of the task.

Ashlee has expressed her extreme frustration about the way that James approaches his work. As a result of this, there is conflict between James and Ashlee, and James is frequently absent from work, which is most likely because he wants to avoid Ashlee.

Scenario 3

Susan and Louise both work in the accounts department. Susan is a very conservative person, who has strong religious beliefs. In contrast, Louise has very liberal views and she is an atheist. She is intolerant of people who are strong supporters of religion.

In their day-to-day work, both Susan and Louise try to steer clear of discussions about religion or politics. However, they are aware of each other's views, and this can cause tension in the office.

The situation comes to a head when Susan arrives at the office wearing a T-shirt showing her support for a conservative political candidate in the upcoming election. Louise feels that Susan has gone too far, as she finds Susan's behaviour confrontational.

Consequences of group conflict

Most of the time we tend to view the consequences of conflict as negative. Although it can be, it can also end up in something positive.

Positive consequences of conflict

- Conflict adds to social alteration, which means both the interpersonal and intergroup dynamics remain new and insightful to current situations.
- Conflict helps the group to explore different options before they make any hasty decision.
- Conflict provides an outlet for members to discuss their interests and differences.
- Conflict will provide an opportunity for everyone to learn from, to be aware and understand each other better, which will strengthen the group unity.

Negative consequences of conflict

- Members get distracted from their primary purpose.
- The conflict can have both physical and psychological health effects on the conflicting parties.
- Members' tolerance for each other might be low. Especially if someone is not doing their part.
- Conflict can cause a breakdown in communication.
- Members' perceptions become distorted, creating negative stereotypes.
- Conflict causes productivity to decrease.
- Members are less motivated to reach their goal.
- Members start seeing each other as enemies.

Figure 3.14 Example of conflict caused by a difference of opinion

3.5.2 Management approach to group conflict

- Hold problem-solving meetings between the conflicting parties, which will provide them with the opportunity to resolve their differences.
- Develop a set of common goals and objectives. This will take the emphasis away from the issues that caused the problem between the conflicting parties.
- If possible, the organisation can increase resources. This will prevent members or groups from competing for limited resources available.
- Management can use smoothing.
- Try to avoid a win-lose situation. Negotiate and bargain in order for conflicting parties to reach some form of agreement or compromise.
- A superior may use his or her formal authority to resolve the conflict if they see it is necessary to intervene.
- Change the behaviour of the members. This is not easy, but it will change stereotypes and attitudes in the long run.
- The organisational structure might not work and be the cause of conflict. Management should redesign or alter the structure to resolve or prevent conflict in the future.
- Provide counselling to parties. Management can use internal or external experts to resolve the conflict.
- It might be necessary to separate the conflicting parties by using them somewhere more suitable.

3.5.3 Effects of cooperation and competition

Cooperation is usually contrasted with competition, but it is important to take note that the two rarely occur separately.

Cooperation is a voluntary process of two or more groups or individuals working together to reach a common goal.

Cooperation in a workplace means that management and employees are working together. Individuals are engaging in open communication, which helps prevent problems before they have a chance to occur. When everyone is working together, everyone can dedicate more time to what he or she needs to do and employees are therefore more productive. They work on a joint action plan in terms of the outputs and results which it will achieve – work is carried out with shared responsibility. This increases cooperation even more and improves job satisfaction. Because employees are asked for their input, the employees feel they are recognised and feel they have a say in the organisation. All employees support one another, which allows the group or team to be more effective.

Figure 3.15 Some effects of cooperation

Competition is a situation or process in which two or more people are on opposing sides, trying to gain or win something.

Competition in the workplace can lead to rivalry among employees. Competition can create stress and defensiveness. Employees are often reluctant to share information and this results in very little communication. This can further lead to serious disagreements or conflict about important issues within the organisation, and results in low productiviety and unhappy employees. However, competition in the workplace can be positive. Healthy competition can be a motivator for employees to perform better and can lead to innovation and creativity, especially if the manager gives honest performace feedback.

Figure 3.16 Some effects of competition

Cooperation is an associated or integrative social process, and competition is a dissociative or disintegrative social process.

See Table 3.3 to understand the significant differences between these two concepts.

Table 3.3 Differences between cooperation and competition

Cooperation	Competition
• Cooperation is a process of people working together for a common goal.	• Competition is a process in which individuals or groups struggle for some goal.
• Qualities like being understanding, selfless and open-minded are necessary.	• Competition has limitations as it is bound by norms.
• Cooperation is limitless. There is no stopping someone helping someone else.	• Constructive competition is always beneficial, but unconstructive competition is harmful.
• Cooperation will give you peace, contentment and a sense of satisfaction.	• Competition may cause both satisfaction and dissatisfaction.
• Cooperation will always be beneficial as it brings a positive result.	• Competition may contribute to the general welfare of the group or organisation.

Competition in the workplace

In the workplace, it is inevitable that there will be some level of competition between co-workers. It might not be an openly stated company policy, but in most companies, competition between fellow workers is encouraged to some extent as co-workers vie for recognition, promotions and performance bonuses. Especially in top level corporations, such as financial companies and legal firms, stiff competition appears to be normal practice.

There is research that shows that competition between employees can be a motivating factor that encourages greater effort, and thus achieves favourable results. Studies have shown that people are more engaged physically and psychologically when they face competition, and so their mind and body are able to perform more effectively.

But we have also seen that people can achieve results in many different ways, some more ethical than others. For example, at Wells Fargo, due to the highly competitive environment and the pressure put on employees to perform, some employees achieved increased sales by covertly creating millions of unauthorised bank and credit card accounts. The eventual outcome of this unethical behaviour was that the company suffered great losses once these practices were exposed.

However, if competition between employees leads to innovation, in which employees find better ways to achieve results or provide services, the competition between the co-workers will have had an extremely positive effect on the way the company operates.

So, what is the difference between competitive situations that compel employees to find solutions in unethical ways and those that encourage positive creative innovations that are of benefit to everyone involved? It depends on how the competition makes employees feel.

If the competition is based on employees' fear of losing their job or being paid less, or of being humiliated in front of their peers, the employees will be acting out of anxiety. On the other hand, if the competition evokes a sense of anticipation in employees as they work towards a bonus or the acknowledgement of their peers or industry, they will be acting out of a sense of excitement.

There is a big difference between these two emotional responses, and they cause people to behave very differently. There is evidence from a number of studies that show when employees experience anxiety as their emotional response to competition, they are less likely to find creative solutions and are more likely to behave unethically. In contrast, when employees experience excitement as their emotional response to competition, they are more likely to exhibit creative behaviour in finding their solutions to the problems, and they are less likely to be unethical.

So, while competition between fellow workers may be an inevitable feature of the workplace, this competition can result in improvements in how the work is done. However, to guarantee an ethical, creative response, employers cannot rely on using fear as the motivating factor.

Read the article above and answer the following questions.

1 Explain each of the following concepts:
   1.1 Group conflict
   1.2 Competition
   1.3 Cooperation
2 Identify five positive and five negative consequences of conflict from the article.

What have we learned about Personnel Management and where to next?

In this module, we learned about group dynamics. We started by discussing what a group is, group development and structure in the workplace. We went on to discuss group effectiveness, group cohesion and the influence in groups. Lastly, we looked at the cooperation and competition within groups, and the effect it has on the workplace.

In the next module, we will learn about leadership.

Revisiting the learning objectives

Now that you have completed this module let's see if you have achieved the learning outcomes that were set out at the beginning of the module. In the table below, we summarise what you have learned for each objective.

Learning objective	What have you learned	✔
Explain what a group is.	A group is two or more individuals interacting with each other to achieve a particular goal. Stages of group formation: • Forming • Storming • Norming • Performing • Adjourning	☐ ☐
Differentiate between formal and informal groups in the workplace.	Formal groups develop deliberately in an organisation to achieve the organisation's goals. Informal groups develop outside the organisation's sphere because the members share the same interest, values, attitudes, etc.	☐ ☐
Explain group formation from perspectives such as groups based on organisational structure, workflow and human needs.	Groups are formed according to: • organisational structure • workflow • human needs	☐
Describe group structure, referring to roles and relationships among the members and the forces that maintain the group's organisation such as leadership and group norms.	Every group that exists has a specific structure. This structure will affect the performance of the group and also create an environment of order. • Group roles • Group interaction • Group leadership • Group norms • Group size • Group status	☐

Explain what groups do for their members to satisfy personal needs.	Effective groups have the following characteristics: • Know their reason for existence • Has guidelines and procedures for decision-making • Members communicate well with each other • Handle conflict constructively • Each member takes responsibility for their actions • Members are loyal to each other • Members trust each other • Members support the performance of others	☐
Explain what groups do for an enterprise to contribute to its success.	Role of the group in the organisation: • Problem-solving • Behavioural standards • Goal-achievement • Leadership development • Group decision-making and performance	☐
Discuss the factors which influence group behaviour and performance. Discuss the advantages and disadvantages of group decisions and performance and how this can be improved.	The advantages of group decision-making: • More information • Diversity of views • Greater acceptability • Expert opinions • Degree of involvement • Communication The disadvantages of group decision-making: • Time-consuming • Individual domination • Pressure • Expensive • Sub-groups	☐ ☐
Explain what is meant by group cohesiveness, how it develops and how it influences group effectiveness.	Cohesion is the degree to which a member is drawn to the group and is motivated to remain a member, forming a united whole.	☐
Discuss the factors which influence group cohesion such as success, group size, stable membership and external threats.	Factors affecting the group cohesiveness: • The size of the group • The work environment • Management style • The group's success • Group status • External threats • Inter- and intra-group competition • Group goals • Lasting relationships	☐
Explain group influence by referring to conformity and social facilitation.	Conformity is the change of the individual's behaviour as a result of the real or imagined pressure of the group. Social facilitation is when a member changes their behaviour as soon as he/she is in the presence of others.	☐ ☐

Explain group conflict, referring to causes and consequences.	Group conflict is an interpersonal problem that occurs between two or more parties.	☐
	What causes group conflict?	
	• Win-lose situation • The method used to achieve the organisational goal • Non-concurring status • Perceptual differences • Change • Interdependence • Limited resources • Reward structures • Communication problems • Other organisational variables	
	The consequences of group conflict	
	Positive consequences of conflict:	
	• Conflict adds to social alteration. • Explore different options before making a decision. • Members discuss their interest and differences. • Everyone learns and understands each other better, this strengthens unity.	☐
	Negative consequences of conflict:	
	• Members get distracted from their main purpose. • Conflict has both physical and psychological health effects. • Members' tolerance for each other might be low. • Conflict can cause a breakdown in communication. • Members' perceptions become distorted. • Conflict causes productivity to decrease. • Members are less motivated to reach their goal. • Members start seeing each other as enemies.	☐
Explain the managerial approach to group conflict.	**What is a management approach to group conflict?**	
	• Hold problem-solving meetings. • Develop a set of common goals and objectives. • Increase the resources. Prevent competing. • Management can use smoothing. • Avoid a win-lose situation. • A superior may use formal authority to resolve the conflict. • Change the behaviour of the members. • The organisational structure might need to be redesigned. • Provide counselling to parties. • Separate the conflicting parties.	☐
Discuss the effects of cooperation and competition.	Cooperation is a voluntary process of two or more groups/individuals working together to reach a common goal.	☐
	Competition is a situation or process in which two or more people are on opposing sides, trying to gain or win something.	☐

Assessment

1. True or false questions

Indicate whether the following statements are TRUE or FALSE. Write only 'true' or 'false' next to the question number.

1.1 Reference groups are when members are different as far as their values and attitudes are concerned.

1.2 Groups set norms for the group as a whole, and the behaviour of the group becomes predictable.

1.3 Interacting and social groups are examples of informal groups.

1.4 Norming is the first stage of group formation and group development.

1.5 The effect that the presence of group members has on the behaviour of individual members is called infirmity.

(5 x 2)

[10]

2. Matching columns

Choose a term from COLUMN B that matches the description in COLUMN A. Write only the letter A, B, C, D or E next to the question number.

	Column A		Column B
2.1	Authority is defined by management	A	Informal group
2.2	Conflict over different objectives	B	Conformity
2.3	The output of one group is the input for another group	C	Cause of conflict
2.4	Supervision is difficult	D	Storming
2.5	The social influence on the individual to change	E	Norm
2.6	Non-concurring status	F	Command (a type of group)
2.7	Semantic differences	G	Interacting group
2.8	Group consisting of superiors and subordinates	H	Formal group
2.9	Friends and family	I	Communication problems
2.10	Accepted standard behaviour	J	Social group

(10 x 2)

[20]

3. Short questions

Answer the following short questions as thoroughly as possible.

3.1 Define the term 'group'. (2)

3.2 Discuss the important impact of informal groups on organisational effectiveness. (5)

3.3 Explain the following:

    3.3.1 Conformity (3)

    3.3.2 Social facilitation (4)

3.4 Name the SIX advantages of group decision-making. (6)

3.5 Name examples of sources for cohesion. (6)

3.6 Name the FOUR roles the group can play in the organisation's success. (4)

[30]

4. Long questions

Answer the following questions in as much detail as possible.

4.1 Discuss FIVE factors of group formation. (5 x 2)

4.2 What are the characteristics of an effective group? (9 x 2)

4.3 Distinguish between a formal and an informal group by using a table. (5 x 2)

4.4 All work groups have a structure that dictates the behaviour of its members and makes the reaching of a group goal possible.
Various factors influence the structure of a group.
Name and explain the factors that influence the structure of a group. (6 x 3)

4.5 Formal groups can be categorised according to the way they interact.
Name and explain these categories. (3 x 2)

4.6 Name and explain the causes of group conflict. (4 x 2)

[70]

Total: [130]

LEADERSHIP

This module covers the following aspects of personnel management:

Unit 4.1	Unit 4.2	Unit 4.3
Approaches to leadership	Leadership styles	Decision-making

Learning objectives

When you have completed this module, you should be able to do the following:

- Define managerial leadership.
- Explain the trait approach to leadership and discuss the implications it has in practice.
- Explain the following behavioural approaches: autocratic leadership, participative leadership and laissez-faire leadership, and discuss the implications it has in practice.
- Explain the functional approach and discuss the implications it has in practice.
- Explain the situational approach and discuss the implications it has in practice.
- Discuss the leaders' manner of acting in the work situation by referring to the following styles: directive, supportive, participative and achievement (task)-orientated.
- Explain what is meant by decision-making in the work practice.
- Explain in a logical manner the steps used in decision-making: analyse the problem, consider the alternative solution, take action – a solution, implement the solution, ongoing evaluation, and modifications.

Key terms

leadership	participative	personal power
theory	authority	decision-making
management	position power	
approach	laissez-faire power	

Starting point

There will always be exceptional leaders in the world, people who inspire many to become the best that they can be. Some leaders lead high profile lives while others inspire and lead the people within their communities. Leaders are people who will be remembered in history as leaders in their field and leaders who made an impact on our lives and the way we see or think about things. Think of people who have inspired you in your life up until now. It could be a famous sportsperson, celebrity, politician, teacher or lecturer.

South Africa's most remarkable and extraordinary leader of all time is Nelson Rolihlahla Mandela (18 July 1918–13 December 2013). Madiba was a lawyer, anti-apartheid revolutionary, a banned person, an ANC and SACP member, MK Commander in Chief, political leader, Nobel Prize winner and the first president of a democratic South Africa from 1994 to 1999. 'Madiba' is known all over the world as one of the greatest leaders of our time. He led with a vision and inspired others to follow his direction to achieve goals. He had compassion, strength and knowledge, and could, therefore, give direction to those following him. His legacy continues to inspire many even after his death. On 18 July every year, we celebrate Mandela Day to honour his legacy. On this day South Africans are inspired to give up their time to help those in need and to continue the legacy of Madiba.

For us to be great leaders, we need to answer a few questions: What makes a great leader? What do leaders do differently than other people to inspire and to gain the respect of so many? In this module, we will be looking at the different approaches to leadership, leadership styles and decision-making. While you work through the module, keep the leaders who have had an influence in your life in mind and see which of the characteristics discussed fits with them.

Figure 4.1 Nelson Mandela, the first president of the new democratic South Africa

UNIT 4.1 Approaches to leadership

4.1.1 Managerial leadership

Both a leader and a manager have a great role to play in any organisation: a leader inspires confidence, trusts, encourages and influence his or her co-workers to work willingly, and guides their activities in an organised effort. On the other hand, a manager is the link between the organisation and its employees, customers, suppliers, shareholders, etc. A manager plans, organises, leads and controls various activities of the organisation towards a specific goal.

Leadership is a critical success factor in any organisation. Therefore, the approach to leadership plays an important and valuable part in determining the success or failure of an organisation.

Over the years a lot of research has been done to attempt to define what leadership is and what qualities, traits and behaviours it has but leadership is hard to define. Leading is one of the four management functions of management, and leadership is the ability to influence a group of people towards setting and achieving goals, which means it is an activity with visible conduct. On the other hand, **management** is the ability to coordinate and organise a group of people and their activities towards achievement of the outlined goals.

Figure 4.2 Management functions

We need a mixture of both leaders and managers to lead organisations in the current business environment. This role style can be called **managerial leadership** – a leader who can reshuffle his or her roles and responsibilities according to the situation to accomplish goals.

Management versus leadership

Managers face many challenges in their capacity as leaders. Leadership is an intricate management activity that incorporates aspects such as authority, power, influence, delegation, responsibility and accountability.

> **DEFINITIONS**
>
> **leadership** – the ability to influence a group of people towards setting and achieving a goal
>
> **management** – the ability to coordinate and organise a group of people and their activities towards achievement of the outlined goals
>
> **managerial leadership** – a leadership style where a leader can reshuffle his or her roles and responsibilities according to the situation to accomplish goals.

Good managers are not necessarily good leaders and good leaders are not necessarily good managers. Management and leaders are two very different concepts, even if they both strive towards the same goal. Their differences lie in their approach to similar challenges.

Table 4.1 highlights the differences between managers and leaders.

Table 4.1 The difference between managers and leaders

Managers	Leaders
• have people who work for them	• have people follow them
• plan and budget	• establish direction
• organise staff	• align people
• control and solve problems	• motivate and inspire
• react to changes	• create change
• communicate	• persuade
• direct groups	• create teams
• try to be heroes	• make heroes of others
• take credit	• take responsibility
• is a formal part of the job description	• inspire by example

As Table 4.1 displayed, a manager knows how to plan, organise and coordinate. When the organisation faces a complex, difficult project, a smart manager knows what to do.

A great leader may know how to influence and motivate people and have wonderful new ideas but may not be so proficient at managing the many ongoing details involved in getting the project done.

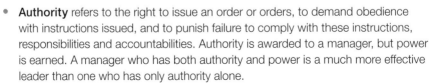

Did you know?

The components of management entail:

- **Authority** refers to the right to issue an order or orders, to demand obedience with instructions issued, and to punish failure to comply with these instructions, responsibilities and accountabilities. Authority is awarded to a manager, but power is earned. A manager who has both authority and power is a much more effective leader than one who has only authority alone.
- **Power** is the manager's ability to influence employees' behaviour. Power is used to persuade employees to direct their time and effort voluntarily towards the accomplishment of the organisation's goals.
- A manager has the **responsibility** and is under the obligation to achieve organisational goals.
- A manager has to **delegate** tasks to employees to assist in achieving organisational goals.
- Managers are held **accountable** for the performance of the team.

In 1959 social psychologists, John French and Betram Raven, divided power into five separate and distinct forms. Let us discuss these five kinds of power:

- Legitimate power. Legitimate power is the authority assigned to a certain post by the organisation. It is the manager's right to enforce carrying out of certain duties and to discuss issues with the employee if they do not comply with these duties. Just because the manager has legitimate power, does not mean he/she is a good leader.

- Reward power. Reward power is the power given to a manager to reward an employee or to withhold a reward. Rewards can be in the form of salary increases, bonuses, recognition or promotion. The greater number of rewards the manager control, the greater is his/her power.
- Coercive power. Coercive power is the ability to enforce submission through fear. The fear can be psychological or physical. Criminal gangs often use coercive power in the form of physical violence.
- Referent power. This power is based on the manager's charisma and/or popularity. Subordinates follow the leader because they like or respect him/her or can identify with him/her. It is the personal traits and characteristics that make him/her attractive.
- Expert power. Expert power is based on expertise, knowledge and personal ability. A leader who possesses this, has certain power over those who have the need for this knowledge or information. The more important the knowledge or information, the more power the individual possess.

A further differentiation must be made between position power and personal power. Position power refers to the formal leadership set up by the organisation's hierarchy from top to bottom. Personal power is the informal leadership which is allocated to a leader, because of his or her personal qualities.

We can also add another source of power, called resource power. Resource power was not included in the initial proposal. At certain times, some people have an influence over others at work, not because of legitimate or personal power, but because of the control they have over the limited available resources.

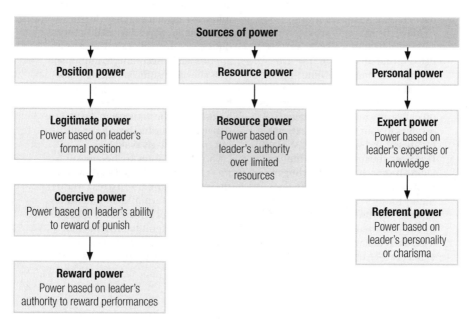

Figure 4.3 The sources of power

Sources: *Organizational Behaviour*, Kreitner & Kinicki, McGraw-Hill.

Leadership and management

Emma works for a non-profit agency that supports children and their families. She is an Associate Director and runs the Programme Evaluation Department, which evaluates the agency's skill-building programmes that are run with families. She reports directly to the general manager of the agency. Because the agency relies on funding from the government, and due to the fact that funding resources are limited, the agency has not been able to recruit new staff this year. However, they have also lost a number of staff members, with two directors, three key research staff and one member of the finance department having left the agency during the year.

Emma's many responsibilities include frequent travel as well as the supervision of two relatively inexperienced managers, both of whom have worked for the agency for less than six months. Each of these managers oversees five members of staff.

One of the managers that Emma supervises is Kathy, who has a background in research. The five members of staff whom she manages provide research support to the Therapeutic Division, which focuses on delivering behavioural health services to youth. Kathy is extremely organised and supports her staff well. However, she frequently exhibits a lack of in-depth understanding of complex issues. The agency values highly Kathy's contributions to recent research on the services delivered by the Therapeutic Division. Kathy is a perfectionist who works hard and expects a lot from herself and her staff.

The other manager supervised by Emma is Linda, who has a strong social science research and evaluation background. The staff she manages work on various projects within the agency. Linda's problem-solving skills are highly valued. She supports her staff very well, and is extremely organised and capable, although she has a tendency to take on too much. The contribution that she makes to the agency with her wealth of experience in the evaluation of family services, is a great asset to the agency.

Kathy and Linda are concerned that the staff working in their teams are becoming overworked as a result of the increased responsibilities they are taking on due to the high turnover of staff. They are also concerned that staff are feeling disheartened, partly as a result of Emma's pessimistic conversational attitude. In addition, Emma has not involved Kathy and Linda in discussions about budgets, and they have not been informed about the budgets for their departments, which has made it very difficult for them allocate work to staff appropriately. According to Emma, she feels she has insufficient information from the finance department to allow her to complete the budgets, but according to the manager of the finance department, she has been given all the information that is available.

Kathy and Linda are becoming increasingly frustrated as they sense their staff members' distress. With the lack of key information about issues such as budget allocations, they are finding it difficult to provide their staff with the support they feel they need or to solve problems that arise.

Form groups of three to five. Read the article above and answer the following questions.

1 How can Emma most effectively use both management and leadership skills in her role as associate director?

2 What could be done by Emma to build staff confidence?
3 What advice would you give Emma on improving her leadership skills and to the managers on developing their management skills?
4 Discuss all the possible answers from all the groups as a class.

4.1.2 Theories of leadership

Leadership **theories** are very complex, and this evolution has been studied for many years. In the beginning the theories focused on the qualities and behaviour of successful leaders. As leadership theories evolved over the years, with a greater understanding of the:

- needs and expectations of the employees/people at work
- impact of a leadership style on those who follow the leader plus the impact of the followers' attitudes, behaviour and skills on the leader
- effectiveness of the different leadership styles in different scenarios or situations.

An **approach** to leadership can be seen as a number of leadership theories classified into one category, because they have similar principles. This classification is important to understand the theories better.

In this section we will be looking at the following four approaches to leadership:

- The trait approach
- The functional approach
- The behavioural approach
- The situational approach.

The trait approach to leadership

The trait approach to leadership is one of the earliest approaches to leadership. It was first proposed by Thomas Carlyle in the 1800's and there have been a number of different studies done since then. This approach is based on the belief that there are a number of personal traits or characteristics that successful leaders possess and share.

In the early 20th century, there were more studies on leadership traits to determine what made certain people great leaders. These theories that were developed were called 'great man' theories because they focused on identifying the qualities and characteristics possessed by great social, political and military leaders.

This unique set of traits is what distinguish effective leaders from non-effective leaders. When you identify and define these characteristics and traits, you can make future predictions of who will be a successful leader.

DEFINITIONS

theory – an explanation for why certain things work and how things materialise; based on an idea that one can test, and not on speculation or a guess

approach – a way of going towards something, to take preliminary steps towards an accomplishment

Studies have identified a number of traits that leaders generally have in common, but it is difficult to pin down a definitive list. Here are some of the traits suggested:

- Physical traits such as above average height and attractiveness
- Intelligence and abilities
- Personality traits, such as adaptability and aggression
- Task relevant traits, such as motivation and initiative
- Social traits, such as interpersonal skills and administrative ability.

This approach suggests that.leaders are 'born' with a number of traits that make them good leaders as opposed to learning leadership behaviour like we will see in the next approach.

The trait approach is different from the other approaches, because it focuses exclusively on the leader, not on the members that follow him or her or the situation.

The behavioural approach to leadership

This approach was developed because of the dissatisfaction with the trait approach to leadership. The behavioural approach states that if we can identify specific leadership behaviours, then we can teach leadership. We can design specific programmes to instil the required behavioural patterns to those who want to be effective leaders.

Several studies emerged in line of this approach. We will focus on the following:

- Lewin's three classical styles of leadership behaviour
- Ohio State Studies
- Blake and Mouton's Leadership Grid

Lewin's three classical styles of leadership behaviour

Lewin suggested three classical styles of leadership. In Table 4.2, the differences between Lewin's three classical styles of leadership are summarised.

Table 4.2 Lewin's three classical leadership styles

	Autocratic	**Participative (Democratic)**	**Laissez-faire**
Description	This style focuses on the power within the leader.	This is also known as the democratic leadership style.	For this style of leadership a policy is nearly non-existent.
	The leader determines his or her own policy and personally gives orders to subordinates. He or she alone make the decisions, set the goals and control the power to reward or punish subordinates' performance. Communication is limited to one way, downward.	The leader will discuss a policy with others and then the group will make a decision. The leader plays the role of facilitator and encourages everyone to participate in the discussions.	The leader participates in discussion to some degree but observe that members of the group work well on their own. Members are given the power to allow freedom of action and there are no interference by the leader.

Nature	Leader retains all authority and responsibility. Leader gives specific tasks to specific people.	Leader delegates authority but maintain responsibility. Tasks are divided.	Leader hand over authority to the group and denies responsibility. Group members must work out things or tasks themselves.
Communication	Downward	Two-way (up- and downward)	Horizontal
Strength	Promptness and order	Develops commitment	Members can do their own thing without interference.
Weakness	Suppress individual initiative	Time consuming	No point of direction

Ohio State Studies

The Ohio State Studies aimed at identifying independent dimensions of leadership. According to these studies, leaders show two dimensions of behaviour which has had an insightful effect on many subsequent leadership theories:

- People-orientated (consideration). This kind of leader is friendly and approachable, and he or she show genuine concern for subordinates' well-being. There is mutual trust, respect for the subordinates' ideas and also a regard for their feelings.
- Initiating structure (task orientation). This kind of leader is characterised by assigning group members to particular tasks and expect them to maintain the standard of performance and meeting the deadlines.

These dimensions in behaviour can further be divided into low or high consideration behaviour, and low or high initiating structure behaviour. See Figure 4.4 below.

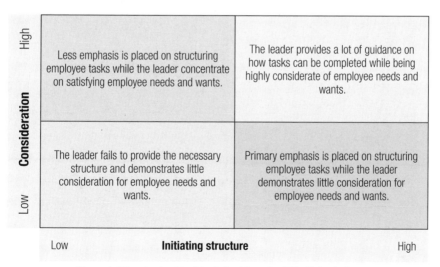

Figure 4.4 Four leadership style derived from the Ohio State studies

A leader showing high initiating structure and high consideration achieves high performances and satisfaction from subordinates. It produces a positive outcome versus that of a leader who is rated low on the two dimensions.

The leadership matrix (grid) of Blake and Mouton

The leadership matrix, also known as the managerial grid, evaluates a leader's behaviour among two dimensions, namely the concern for production and the concern for people. This essentially represent the Ohio States dimensions of considerations and initiating structure.

The leadership grid is a useful mechanism to enable leaders to identify their own assumptions about people and the job to be done. By knowing the style of other leaders and their own leadership style, they will be more set to appraise objectively, to communicate better, to understand where differences originate and to assist other in being more productive.

Blake and Mouton identified three general traits of organisations:

* Every organisation has its own goals to pursue. This will determine the job to be done.
* No organisation can function without people.
* Every organisation has a hierarchy of authority.

The relation between these three traits is the foundation on what the leadership grid is built on. The grid has nine possible positions along each axis, from low (point 1) through average (point 5) to high (point 9), creating 81 (9 x 9) different positions in which the leader's style fall. See Figure 4.5 on the next page.

The Leadership Grid Figure

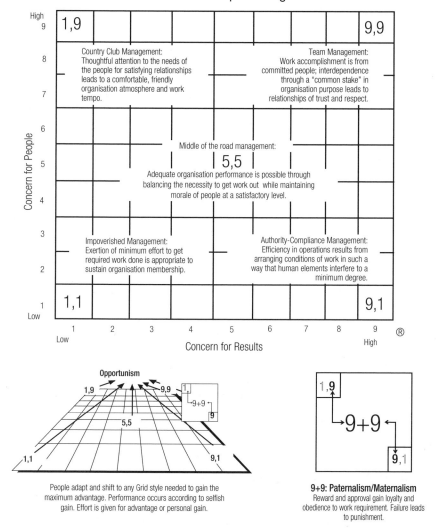

Figure showing the Leadership Grid with axes "Concern for People" (vertical) and "Concern for Results" (horizontal):

1,9 – Country Club Management: Thoughtful attention to the needs of the people for satisfying relationships leads to a comfortable, friendly organisation atmosphere and work tempo.

9,9 – Team Management: Work accomplishment is from committed people; interdependence through a "common stake" in organisation purpose leads to relationships of trust and respect.

5,5 – Middle of the road management: Adequate organisation performance is possible through balancing the necessity to get work out while maintaining morale of people at a satisfactory level.

1,1 – Impoverished Management: Exertion of minimum effort to get required work done is appropriate to sustain organisation membership.

9,1 – Authority-Compliance Management: Efficiency in operations results from arranging conditions of work in such a way that human elements interfere to a minimum degree.

Opportunism

People adapt and shift to any Grid style needed to gain the maximum advantage. Performance occurs according to selfish gain. Effort is given for advantage or personal gain.

9+9: Paternalism/Maternalism
Reward and approval gain loyalty and obedience to work requirement. Failure leads to punishment.

Figure 4.5 The leadership grid

Source: The Leadership Grid ® figure, Paternalism Figure and Opportunism from Leadership Figure 4.5 The leadership grid Dilemmas--Grid Solutions, by Robert R. Blake and Anne Adams McCanse (Formerly the Managerial Grid by Robert R. Blake and Jane S. Mouton). Houston: Gulf Publishing Company, (Grid Figure: P. 29, Paternalism Figure: p. 30, Opportunism Figure: p. 31). Copyright 1991 by Scientific Methods, Inc. Reproduced by permission of the owners.

Look at a few more examples of managers and their positions on the leadership grid in Table 4.3 to explain this further.

Table 4.3 Some more examples of managers on the leadership grid

Position	Kind of manager	Description
1,1	The impoverished manager	• This manager has a low concern for production and a low concern for people. The manager do not interfere. • *Laissez-faire leadership.* The leader does the minimum required.
1,9	The country club manager	• This manager has a high concern for production and a low concern for people. • *Democratic leadership.* Maintaining sound interpersonal relationships will be most important.
9,1	The authority compliance manager	• This manager has a high concern for production and a low concern for people. • *Autocratic leadership.* Production is achieved by means of formal authority, and subordinates being submissive.
5,5	The middle-of-the-road manager	• This manager try to balance the need to achieve results, while maintaining the morale and satisfaction of the employee. • *Organisation leadership.* The leader try unenthusiastically to pay attention to both aspects, but does not succeed.
9,9	The team manger	• This manager has a high commitment to the objectives of the organisation as well as satisfying the needs of the employee. • *Team leadership.* The leader focuses on team-work.

Power Break 4.2   INDIVIDUAL WORK

Read the article below and answer the following questions.

A remarkable turnaround

Carol Baines was married for 20 years to the owner of the Baines Company until he died in a car accident. After his death, Carol decided not to sell the business but to try to run it herself. Before the accident, her only involvement in the business was in informal discussions with her husband over dinner, although she has a college degree in business, with a major in management.

Baines Company was one of three office supply stores in a city with a population of 200,000 people. The other two stores were owned by national chains. Baines was not a large company and employed only five people. Baines had stable sales of about $200,000 a year, serving mostly the smaller companies in the city. The firm had not grown in a number of years and was beginning to feel the pressure of the advertising and lower prices of the national chains.

For the first 6 months, Carol spent her time familiarising herself with the employees and the operations of the company. Next, she did a citywide analysis of companies that had reason to purchase office supplies. Based on her understanding of the company's capabilities and her assessment of the potential market for their products and services, Carol developed a specific set of short-term and long-term goals for the company.

Behind all of her planning, Carol had a vision that Baines could be a viable, healthy, and competitive company. She wanted to carry on the business that her husband had started, but more than that she wanted it to grow. Over the first 5 years, Carol invested significant amounts of money in advertising, sales, and services. These efforts were well spent because the company began to show rapid growth immediately. Because of the growth, the company hired another 20 people.

The expansion at Baines was particularly remarkable because of another major hardship Carol had to confront. Carol was diagnosed with breast cancer a year after her husband died. The treatment for her cancer included 2 months of radiation therapy and 6 months of strong chemotherapy. Although the side effects included hair loss and fatigue, Carol continued to manage the company throughout the ordeal. Despite her difficulties, Carol was successful. Under the strength of her leadership, the growth at Baines continued for 10 consecutive years.

Interviews with new and old employees at Baines revealed much about Carol's leadership. Employees said that Carol was a very solid person. She cared deeply about others and was fair and considerate. They said she created a family-like atmosphere at Baines. Few employees had quit Baines since Carol took over. Carol was devoted to all the employees, and she supported their interests. For example, the company sponsored a softball team in the summer and a basketball team in the winter.

Others described Carol as a strong person. Even though she had cancer, she continued to be positive and interested in them. She did not get depressed about the cancer and its side effects, even though coping with cancer was difficult. Employees said she was a model of strength, goodness, and quality.

At age 55, Carol turned the business over to her two sons. She continues to act as the president but does not supervise the day-to-day operations. The company is doing more than $3.1 million in sales, and it outpaces the other two chain stores in the city.

Source: *Trait Approach*, P. Northouse, SAGE Publishers

1 How would you describe Carol's leadership traits?
2 How big a part did Carol's traits play in the expansion of the company?
3 Would Carol be a leader in other business contexts?
4 Would you describe Carol as an autocratic, democratic or laissez-faire leader? Give a reason or reasons for your answer.
5 What do you see as Carol's strength and weakness?
6 Use the leadership grid to evaluate Carol's behaviour. Give Carol a number, for example 4,8 (4 on the people concern and 8 on the results concern lines), which will best describe her.

The functional approach to leadership

This approach was developed as a result of the shortcomings of other studies. Researchers realised that a leader cannot achieve anything in isolation. Leaders are dependent on their followers.

The functional approach sees leadership as consisting of a number of essential functions that have to be performed. These functions are not restricted to the leader performing all the functions. Workers can learn, develop and perfect these skills of leadership. Those workers with the potential for leadership are exposed to experiences designed to develop that potential.

A study by Krech *et al.* in Mullins (1999:263) identify the functions of a leader as summarised in Table 4.4.

Table 4.4 Functions of a leader

Leadership function	Description
Executive	Leaders coordinates group activities and make sure of the application of the policies.
Planner	Leaders determine the ways and means by which groups achieve their goal.
Policy maker	Leaders define the goals and objectives of the group.
External group representative	Leaders are the voice of the group and also the filter through which both incoming and outgoing information is channelled.
Controller of internal relations	Leaders determine the internal arrangement and structure for working in a group.
Controller of internal rewards and punishment	Leaders have the power and authority to reward or to punish workers.
Arbitrator and mediator	Leaders control the way internal conflict in the group is handled.
Role model	Leaders are the ones that set an example for the others in the group to see.
Symbol of the group	Leaders give direction by providing mental focus and improve unity by distinguishing the group as a unique entity.
Substitute for individual responsibility	Leaders let individual members go of the need for personal decision-making.
Father figure	Leaders are the source of stability and instil positive emotional feelings for individual members,
Scapegoat	Leaders are the punching bag and target for the aggression and hostility of the group if they experience failure. Leaders will also take the blame for such failure. ·

The situational approach to leadership

Situational approach to leadership is also known as the 'life cycle theory of leadership'. This approach focuses on leadership in different situations. Each different situation demands a different type of leadership. This approach has a supportive and a directive dimension. For the leader to be effective, he/she has to be able to recognise what employees need and to change their style to satisfy those needs.

There are several situational leadership models. We shall discuss the following two:

- The Situational Leadership® Model (developed by Paul Hersey)
- Theory X and Theory Y (Douglas McGregor).

The Situational Leadership® Model

This model is based on the relationship between leaders and the individual or group they are attempting to influence (lead) and serves as a framework to analyse each situation based on:

- The amount of guidance and direction (task behaviour) a leader gives
- The amount of socio-emotional support (relationship behaviour) a leader provides
- The Performance Readiness® Level that followers exhibit in performing a specific task, function of an objective.

In essence, leaders using the Situational Leadership® Model (see Figure 4.6) start with the task and the person responsible for performing it, then ask: How much task-specific

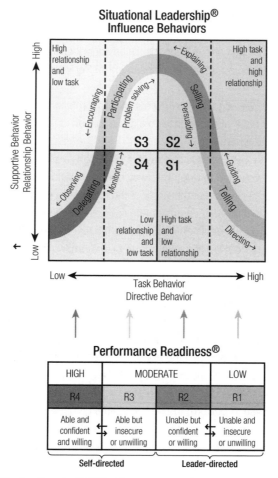

Figure 4.6 Hersey's Situational Leadership® Model
Source: Situational Leadership® and Performance Readiness® are registered trademarks of Leadership Studies, Inc. Copyright © 1972 - 2017. All Rights Reserved.

knowledge, experience or skill does this person bring to the table? Is this individual confident, committed and motivated to perform this task?

Answers to these simple questions produce four combinations of ability and willingness (Performance Readiness®) that the leader can use as a starting point:

- R1 – "I need clear structure and direction."
- R2 - "I am inexperienced but highly motivated, so I need both encouragement and direction."
- R3 - "I have a good understanding of what to do, but I need support."
- R4 - "I am motivated, competent and confident."

The leader then determines leadership style as a function of:

- **Task behaviour.** The degree to which the leader provides directions for the tasks of the group members by indicating who should do what, when, where and how. Task behaviour is characterised by a leader establishing organisational patterns, channels of communication and procedures for the execution of tasks.
- **Relationship behaviour.** The degree to which the leader engages in interpersonal relationships between themselves and members of the group. Leaders provide open channels for communication, support and encouragement.

Various combinations of task and relationship behaviour define four leadership styles the leader can employ depending upon the assessment of Performance Readiness® for the task in question:

- Telling or guiding (S1) – High task behaviour plus low relationship behaviour. The leader relies on his or her base of experience to explain to individuals or the group what to do, how, where and when.
- Selling or explaining (S2) High task behaviour plus high relationship behaviour. The leader guides subordinates through two-way communication, e.g. the leader clarifies decisions and recognises the enthusiasm of the follower to ensure understanding.
- Participating or involving (S3) Low task behaviour plus high relationship behaviour. Subordinates take part in decision-making with the leader through two-way communication, e.g. both parties take part in brainstorming alternatives to mutually establish alignment.
- Delegating or entrusting (S4) Low task behaviour plus low relationship behaviour. The leader trusts the follower to rely on his or her base of experience to take independent decisions and to complete the task with the necessary confidence and willingness.

Leadership effectiveness depends on a leader's ability to assess the Performance Readiness® of an individual and use the appropriate leadership style for the situation. For example, a new employee with little knowledge and experience to perform a task would require more direction than an employee who has several years of experience. If a leader entrusts a new employee to perform the task with little guidance, then the employee will likely exhibit poor performance and ultimately feel frustrated and lost. However, if a leader provides proper detail and instruction, then the employee will feel empowered with the knowledge to effectively perform the task. However, a leader cannot merely provide direction without also providing some level of support. How much is some? It indeed depends on the situation, which is precisely what the Situational Leadership® Model helps leaders to determine.

Theory X and Theory Y – Douglas McGregor

A final discussion about situational leadership, we study Douglas McGregor's research. According to McGregor, leaders (managers) make certain assumptions about their co-workers, peers and subordinates. Their assumptions are reflected in the way they treat or behave towards these individuals.

McGregor compiled two opposing views about the assumptions which may affect a leader's behaviour. The two sets of assumptions are summarised in Table 4.5, listed as Theory X and Theory Y:

Table 4.5 Assumptions for Theory X and Theory Y

Theory X	Theory Y
People are fundamentally lazy and will avoid work if possible.	Work is as natural as play or rest.
People are extrinsically motivated and rate security above any other need.	People are intrinsically motivated and seek self-actualisation.
People are incapable of self-discipline and self-control. People prefer to be controlled and not to take responsibility and have no ambition.	People apply self-discipline and self-control. People seek opportunities to take responsibility.
Most people have limited creativity when they try to solve organisational problems.	Being creative when solving organisational problem is a general occurrence.

McGregor put a strong emphasis on the importance to integrate individual goals with the goals of the organisation and to find the best suited leadership style to reach these goals.

He had a lot of criticism about his theory, but it had a major impact on the modern concept of leadership.

Power Break 4.3 GROUP WORK

Leadership is the process of influencing and directing the behaviours of others (employees) to achieve organisational goals. Blake and Mouton, through the managerial grid, were looking for the ideal leadership style while Hersey and Blanchard focus on the situation that will determine the style of the leader.

Reread the paragraph above and discuss leadership by answering the following questions.

1 Name and explain the position powers of a leader.
2 Except for the position powers named in QUESTION 1, name the other types of power included.
3 With the aid of a diagram, discuss Hersey and Blanchard's situational leadership style in detail. The discussion must focus on both the leadership styles as well as the maturity levels of the subordinates.

UNIT 4.2 **Leadership styles**

There are four main leadership styles. A leadership style refers to the leader's characteristic behaviours when he or she is directing, motivating, guiding, and managing followers. Leadership also provide followers direction for implementing plans.

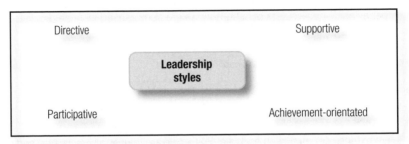

Figure 4.7 The four main leadership styles

4.2.1 Directive leadership style

- Directive leadership style is characterised by clear objectives and rules for the followers. A command and control style.
- The expectations and directions are clearly defined and understood.
- This leadership style may be applied when subordinates/followers are unskilled or inexperienced.
- This is also a good leadership style within a business where followers have jobs that are not particular specialised.
- Subordinates or followers still need clear directions, guidance to avoid uncertainty, especially when it is a complex task.
- Directive leadership style may not be a good idea to imposed upon highly skilled and experience employees. They are already extremely competent to perform the task. It may backfire negatively on the leader.
- The positives of this type of leadership style are that it provides structure to unstructured tasks and it creates clarity within role expectations.
- The downside to this leadership style is that it restricts initiative and not being part of any decision-making.

Did you know?

When is the best time or situation to use directive leadership?

- When team members are unskilled.
- When there is an urgency, emergency or crisis.
- When you need team members to follow the rules.
- When the leader needs to make quick decisions.

Figure 4.8 The directive leadership style has clear objectives and rules.

4.2.2 Supportive leadership style

- Supportive leadership style is a leadership style where a leader or manager is not just interested in giving orders and receiving results.
- Supportive leaders give the subordinates the tools they need to work themselves and support them until the task is completed.
- See the illustration below of the difference between a traditional vs. supportive leader:

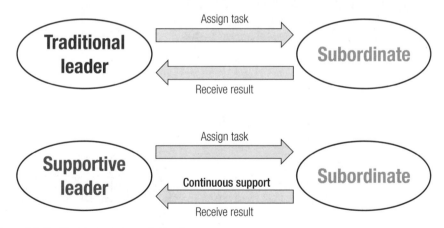

Figure 4.9 Traditional versus supportive leader

- The upside to this style is that the manager works with the subordinate until he or she is empowered and skilled enough to do the work on their own or with minimum supervision.
- Supportive leadership style involves building trust, inspiration, and helping subordinates to overcome challenges they may encounter.
- This leadership style is however not applicable for all organisations. In organisations where the tasks are straightforward and simple, it might be a waste of time.

Figure 4.10 The supportive leadership style involves trust, inspiration and helping subordinates to overcome challenges.

4.2.3 Participative leadership style

- Participative leadership style is also known as a democratic leadership style.
- This style of leadership involves the followers in the decision-making process. Followers are allowed to give their input, although the final decision-making authority remain that of the leader.
- To use this leadership style should not be seen as a sign of weakness, but rather a strength and shows mutual respect for each other.
- Participative leadership style is normally used when you have part of the information, and your employees have the other parts. You as a

Figure 4.11 The participate leadership style involves both the leader and his or her followers in the decision-making process.

leader is not expected to know everything all the time – this is why you appoint people with knowledge and skills.

- Using this style is beneficial for both the leader and the followers. Followers will feel part of the team, they will feel their input are valued and it will build their self-confidence. From the leader's perspective, he or she will make better, more informed decisions.
- The followers' answers and feedback will give the leader a greater perspective, more diverse and creative ways of solving the problem.

4.2.4 Achievement (task) -oriented leadership style

- This leadership style focuses on high performance. The leader has a high level of confidence in the employee's ability to achieve the goals.
- Instead of being focused on the people doing the work, leaders practicing this style are focused on what is being achieved by their teams.
- The focus is always on making it to the end of the project instead of focusing on what people bring to the task.
- Everyone on a team tends to be on the same page to a greater extent when achievement-oriented leadership is being used. That is because the goal is the outcome which needs to be achieved. To make outcomes happen, leaders must be able to outline specific tasks and steps that the team must take.
- Leaders who are focused on achievements tend to avoid receiving any sort of feedback from their team. There is a tendency to demand that each step be completed in the way that was outlined for each worker, which eliminates the ability for someone to improve upon the process.

Figure 4.12 The achievement leadership style focuses on the end of the project.

Jeremy is a grocer store manager

The world's third-largest retailer, groceries and general merchandise retailer Grocer, is a multinational store with its headquarters in England.

Jeremy manages a medium-sized Grocer store. He started working for the company more than 10 years as a shelf-filler in the dairy section and now he is working towards the Grocer foundation degree. Jeremy works with a team of about 20 departmental managers, who in turn manage almost 300 people. As a leader, Jeremy generally allows his managers to make most operational decisions, unless he has reason to step in. For example, if an accident occurs in the store, Jeremy might take over the management of the incident to make sure it is dealt with swiftly and efficiently.

There are many different styles of leadership.

- In some approaches, the manager allows his or her team to participate up to a point, while reserving the right to make the final decision.

- Managers who adopt an 'I sell' approach try to persuade all the members of their teams that their viewpoint is the one that must be accepted.

- Managers who adopt an 'I consult' approach, seek the opinions of team members before they make a decision, which is closer to a democratic style of management.

Good managers adapt their leadership style to be appropriate in the circumstances. Jeremy consults his staff on most issues, as he feels that they respond better to this style of leadership. For example, when the team plans a campaign or programme, he asks the managers to put forward ideas and gets their help with the development of plans. This approach motivates the team and encourages creativity. Even if mistakes are made, Jeremy draws on them to inform the learning process.

As a manager of a store, Jeremy has to deal with a wide variety of situations, and some of these will be critical to the business. In these cases, it is vital that Jeremy responds in the most appropriate way to the situation at hand and he may need to adapt his leadership style to one in which he exerts his authority and deals with the situation with less input from the team.

Read the article above and answer the following questions.

1 What leadership style do you think Jeremy used in general? Explain your answer.
2 What are the advantages of this leadership style?
3 What leadership style would you associate with an 'I sell' philosophy and an 'I consult' approach?
4 Do you think Jeremy's leadership style is the best possible style for his position?

Bill Gates

Born in the USA in 1955, Bill Gates is a highly admired business leader and also one of the best-known. He achieved great success as one of the founding partners of the computer software company Microsoft, which he launched with his friend Paul Allen in 1975. The company was listed on the American stock exchange in 1981.

The young Bill Gates was fascinated by computers. He started programming mainframe computers at the age of thirteen. He went on to attend Harvard University, where he developed an adaptation of the BASIC programming language for use on personal computers.

Gates recognised the potential of the personal computer, and realised that it could take off in popularity worldwide if people could afford it. He believed that computers would become much more affordable over time. Therefore, he predicted that there would come a time when most people would have their own computer. The great success that he achieved in building his software development company, Microsoft, is evidence of the accuracy of his prediction, and he went on to become one of the world's wealthiest persons.

Bill Gates retired from Microsoft in 2008, but is still highly respected in the world of commerce. In the workplace, Gates expected high standards from his employees. He values creativity and innovation very highly. He also acknowledges individuals and teams who achieve good results.

As chairman of Microsoft, he regularly asked employees to share their work with him, to inform him about what they were working on and what new ideas they had. He participated actively in these presentations, often challenging or asking for more information about the ideas people shared with him.

Read the article above and answer the following questions.

1 What is the leadership style used by Bill Gates? Explain your answer.
2 It is unlikely that Gates would have been as successful as he was if he only ever adopted one leadership style. Which other leadership styles, depending on the situation, would you recommend Bill Gates use? Give reasons for your answer.

UNIT 4.3 Decision-making in the work practice

4.3.1 What is decision-making in the work practice?

In Module 3 we discussed the concept of decision-making. Please refer to Unit 3.2.4. In this section we discuss what decision-making is, the key elements of decision-making and the steps to follow in making a well-informed decision.

The term decision-making refers to the process of deciding about something important, especially in an organisation. Decision-making is choosing among two or more possible alternatives or paths for a given situation.

Making decisions is part of the daily tasks of an organisation. Every level of management at some stage have to make a decision. It is important for every manager to make the correct decision in order to reach the organisation's goals. These decisions vary from minor decisions to major decisions that can have a minor to catastrophic outcome if an incorrect decision is made.

Decisions we make have the potential to affect ourselves and others in the short and long run. For example, an organisation needs to make the following decision with regards to their plant, products and personnel:

- Plant – Should the organisation invest in a new factory or upgrading their current one?
- Products – Should they introduce new products, or should they invest in modernising their current products?
- Personnel – Should they introduce computerised systems or train their current personnel to be better equipped?

The key elements in decision-making

- **The concept of the best decision.** The problem at hand should be thoroughly analysed and all the possible alternatives should be considered.
- **The environment of the organisation.** The organisation itself has a great influence on decision-making. Some organisations rely on rigid centralisation (from one central point, e.g. top management) in their approach to decision-making. Others have faith in decentralisation and trust the different levels of management to make routine decisions.
- **Psychological elements in decision-making.** Traits like intellectual maturity, experience, education, religion, habits, social status, etc., can all influence your decision.
- **The timing of your decision.** To make the right decision at the right time. The timing of your decision is as important as making the right decision.
- **Communicate the decision taken.** It is important to communicate your decision to everyone it may concern and influence. Supervisors should inform subordinates about the decision they made if it concerns them, for example if management is going to close down a department. When everyone is informed, it prevents information via the grapevine.
- **Participation of employees.** The concept of two heads are better than one applies here. Getting inputs from employees will ensure a more efficient and informed decision. Employees giving their inputs will also feel they are valued and part of the 'team'.

4.3.2 The steps in the decision-making process

Decision-making is the process of making choices by identifying a decision, gathering information, and assessing alternative solutions

To make this process easier and more accurate, you can use a step-by-step decision-making process. This process will help you to make a more informed and thoughtful decision.

Figure 4.13 Making a thoughtful decision

Table 4.6 The decision-making process

1	Analyse the problem	
	Identify the decision	Clearly define the decision you must make and analyse the importance for you to solve it.
	Gather information	Gather relevant information before you make a decision. Gather information from the internal and external environment.
	Analyse the situation	Leaders should fully understand the problem or situation before they consider different alternatives.
2	Consider the alternative solutions	
	Identify and evaluate alternatives	As you gather information, you will identify several possible paths of action, or alternatives. List all possible and desirable alternatives.
3	Take action – a solution	
	Choose among alternatives	Leaders must make the final decision as to which alternative they choose and apply.
	Set criteria to evaluate	Evaluate the alternative against a pre-set criterion to determine whether the problem will effectively be addressed.
	Determine the consequences	Do a risk analysis to determine the possible consequences of each of the alternatives.
	Take action	You are now ready to take action, to make a decision – choose the alternative that will best resolve the problem.

> **DEFINITION**
>
> **decision-making** – the process of making choices by identifying a decision, gathering information, and assessing alternative solutions

4	Implement the solution	
	Implement the solution	Implement the decision by planning the activities to follow.
5	Ongoing evaluation	
	Evaluate effectiveness of your decision	Review your decision, the results, to make sure the problem is resolved and that the decision was the correct one. If you achieved the outcome, it is great, and you might want to reflect upon what went right, any challenges encountered and the lessons learned.
6	Modifications	
	Implement Plan B	If you have not achieved the outcome, you may need to find out why the outcome was not achieved. You may want to refer back to the previous stage of the decision-making process to gather more information and explore other alternatives.

Figure 4.14 The complete process of decision-making

Power Break 4.6　INDIVIDUAL WORK

Read the article below.

Making decisions

Sue Britz is 22 years of age and will receiving her Human Resources diploma from College of South Africa at the end of this year. She spends the last 18 months working for YMS Insurance, a well-established organisation, doing her internship. She has received an offer to join YMS Insurance on a permanent basis as the HR assistant. The job description is very similar to what she had be doing the last 18 months.

She enjoyed her internship and build good relationship with the management and other colleagues. She will receive a good salary plus benefits. Ms. Jones, the current HR manager is 55 years old and settled in her position. She won't apply for other positions, which means Sue will only be promoted later (and that is never a given) in her career. Ms Jones is very good mentor and got lots of experience to learn from.

Sue was also offered a permanent HR position at Mark's Logistics, a new courier company, as the HR manager. They offered Sue a similar salary as YMS Insurance, but with no benefits. Sue will be in charge of the human resources department. Mark's Logistics also offered her a 5% share in the company after five years. She will still receive a salary increase every year and a bonus each year if the company is doing well.

Use the following worksheet to evaluate the case study.

Worksheet	
1 Identify Sue's problem.	
2 What are Sue's choices?	
3 Gather information: What information available and what information should Sue gather that would be helpful to know before making a decision?	
4 Consider the outcome. What would be the results of her decision?	
5 Make the decision. What do you think Sue should do?	
6 Why do you think this is the best decision possible?	

What have we learned about Personnel Management and where to next?

In this module, we learned about leadership. We started by discussing managerial leadership, approaches to leadership and leadership styles. Lastly, we looked at decision-making in the work practice and the steps used in decision-making.

In the next module, we will learn about information systems and graphic representations for managing human resources.

Revisiting the learning objectives

Now that you have completed this module let's see if you have achieved the learning outcomes that were set out at the beginning of the module. In the table below, we summarise what you have learned for each objective.

Learning objective	What have you learned	✔
Define managerial leadership.	• **Leadership** is the ability to influence a group of people towards setting and achieving a goal. • **Management** is the ability to coordinate and organise a group of people and their activities towards achievement of the outlined goals. • **Managerial leadership** is a leadership style where a leader can reshuffle his or her roles and responsibilities according to the situation to accomplish goals.	☐ ☐ ☐

Explain the following theories of leadership:
 	
• the trait approach
• the behavioural approach
  – autocratic leadership
  – participative leadership
  – laissez-faire leadership
• the functional approach
• the situational approach
Discuss the implications these theories of leadership have in practice.
	Theories (approaches) of leadership:
	
	• Trait approach is based on the belief that there are a number of personal traits that successful leaders possess.
	• Behavioural approach beliefs that if we can identify specific leadership behaviours, we can teach leadership.
	• Refer to Table 4.2, Figure 4.4 and Figure 4.5.
	• The functional approach sees leadership as consisting of a number of essential functions that have to be performed. These functions are not restricted to the leader performing all the functions. Workers can learn, develop and perfect these skills of leadership.
	• Situational approach to leadership is also known as the 'life cycle theory of leadership'. This approach focuses on leadership in different situations. Each different situation demands a different type of leadership. This approach has a supportive and a directive dimension.
	     Refer to Figure 4.6.
		☐
		☐
		☐
		
		☐
		
		☐

Discuss the leaders' manner of acting in the work situation by referring to the following styles: • directive • supportive • participative • achievement (task)-orientated.	• A leadership style refers to the leader's characteristic behaviours when he/she is directing, motivating, guiding, and managing followers. Leadership styles: • Directive leadership style is characterised by clear objectives and rules for the followers. A command and control style. • Supportive leadership style is a leadership style where a leader or manager is not just interested in giving orders and receiving results. • Participative leadership style is also known as a democratic leadership style. This style of leadership the leader involves the followers in the decision-making process. • Achievement-oriented leadership style focuses on high performances. Leaders have a high level of confidence in the employee's ability to achieve the goals.	☐ ☐ ☐ ☐ ☐
Explain what is meant by decision-making in the work practice.	Decision-making refers to the process of deciding about something important, especially in an organisation. Decision-making is choosing among two or more possible alternatives/paths for a given situation.	☐
Explain in a logical manner the steps used in decision-making: analyse the problem • consider the alternative solution • take action – a solution • implement the solution • ongoing evaluation • modifications.	Key elements in decision-making: • The concept of the best decision. • The environment of the organisation. • Psychological elements in decision-making. • The timing of your decision. • Communicate the decision taken • Participation of employees. The decision-making process: • Identify the decision • Gather information • Analyse the situation • Identify alternatives • Evaluate alternatives • Choose among alternatives • Set criteria to evaluate • Determine the consequences • Implement your decision • Evaluate effectiveness of your decision	☐ ☐

Assessment

1. True or false questions

Indicate whether the following statements are TRUE or FALSE. Write only 'true' or 'false' next to the question number.

	Statement	True	False
1.1	The leader of a gang will be the one who is less aggressive and physical weak.		
1.2	Leadership is used enthusiastically and effectively in order to accomplish the organisational objectives.		
1.3	Blake and Mouton's leadership grid model is not in favour of supportive management but believes in enforcement.		
1.4	A leader is not able to manage conflict fairly.		
1.5	Power is evident in a person that possess authority or influence.		

(5 x 2)

[10]

2. Multiple-choice questions

Choose the correct answer from the various options provided. Write only A, B or C next to the question number.

2.1 An autocratic leader ...

    A takes charge and assumes full authority and responsibility.

    B shows concerns for production.

    C emphasises group cohesiveness.

    D is participative. (2)

2.2 An example of a democratic leader, is ...

    A Hitler

    B Robert Mugabe

    C Nelson Mandela

    D Julius Ceasar (2)

2.3 Referent power is based on ...

    A the power to enforce subordinates to carry out duties.

    B the manager's charisma.

    C managers' ability to reward employees.

    D the manager's expertise. (2)

2.4 Laissez-faire communicate ...

    A downward

    B upward

    C horizontal

    D none of the above (2)

2.5 Which one of the following is NOT a leadership trait?

    A   Conservative

    B   Sociability

    C   Resilience

    D   Determined   (2)

    (5 x 2)

    [10]

3. Short questions

Briefly answer the following questions.

3.1 Explain the term leadership. (3)

3.2 Name the four main management functions. (4)

3.3 Briefly name and explain five essential functions according to Krech. (5 x 2)

3.4 Name the three general traits identified by Blake and Mouton. (3)

    [20]

4. Long questions

Answer the following questions as comprehensively as you can.

4.1 What are the NINE qualities, characteristics or traits a person should have to be a successful leader? (9)

4.2 Explain the different leadership styles according to Blake and Mouton's managerial grid. (5 x 4)

4.3 Differentiate between a leader and a manager. (5 x 2)

4.4 Discuss the difference between Theory X and Theory Y. (4 x 2)

4.5 Discuss the six main leadership styles. (6 x 3)

    [65]

    Total: [105]

INFORMATION SYSTEMS AND GRAPHIC REPRESENTATIONS FOR MANAGING HUMAN RESOURCES

This module covers the following aspects of personnel management:

Unit 5.1	**Unit 5.2**
Computerised information systems (CIS)	Spreadsheets and graphic representations

Learning objectives

When you have completed this module, you should be able to do the following:

- Discuss the aims and objectives of human resources information (data) systems (HRIS) in the work environment.
- Explain the advantages of computerised information systems in practice.
- Describe the procedures (task list) for the design, development (steps) and the implementation and evaluation of effective human resource management systems briefly.
- List software packages with prepacked personnel systems to be used in practice and criteria to evaluate them.
- Describe the content of the two major classes of information, namely organisational and employee information, under the following:
  - Performance appraisal
  - Salary administration
  - Health and safety
  - Education and training
  - Payroll
  - Employment/recruitment
  - Benefits administration
- Demonstrate the use of spreadsheets and graphs to provide information for management.
- Demonstrate the use of graphics presentations to provide information for management.

Key terms

data	information	MIS
HRIS	controlled access	user-friendly
performance management	payroll	spreadsheet

Starting point

Organisations operate in a very dynamic environment. The world around the organisation has and is still undergoing significant change. These changes also influence the way in which organisations function within themselves. Technology has become a vital part of our lives, and one cannot imagine life without it.

HRIS @ Nissan: A New Era in Human Resource Management

Information is the most vital part of the survival or growth of the firm. Today human resource has become the main competitive advantage for a firm, making it a very critical resource. More so than ever, there is a need for fulfilling all functions related to the human resource with strategic purpose and technology should be able to help in aligning them with the firm's objectives. Human Resource Information Systems (HRIS) are one such technological innovation which can efficiently help in standardising such information about company's employees.

"Our strategy was not just to develop HR shared services; it was to transform human resources throughout the entire company, to add more to the business." - Dwain Stevens, Sr. HR Manager, Nissan.

Nissan Motors, one of the top-selling automobile manufacturers and the world's first ever multi-brand conglomerate after its collaboration with Renault, has over 130,000 people working for them worldwide. This global corporation needed standardised HR practices in order to function successfully. The firm was also concerned about the overall employee satisfaction. Having an HRIS meant a strategic investment to reduce costs across the globe, and therefore, in 2010, CEO Carlos Ghosn introduced HRIS in Nissan, when Nissan was in troubled waters. His aim was not only to automate the HR services but to transform HR services in the whole organisation.

Source: 'HRIS at Nissan: A new era in human resource management', January 2013, International Journal of Teaching and Case Studies 4(2): 95-114

Figure 5.1 HRIS @ Nissan

UNIT 5.1 Computerised Information Systems

In Starting point, you saw how organisations need to collect and store large amounts of **data** relating to the Human Resource function. This includes important details such as employee identity numbers, tax numbers, start dates, salary scales, etc.

The Human Resource department is responsible for organising, processing and interpreting this data to create useful **information.** Managers use this information to make informed decisions that will contribute towards achieving departmental and organisational objectives.

The process of converting data into information can be streamlined by using computer technology together with software applications such as **Management Information Systems (MIS)**. The MIS is the application of information technology to serve the business and it forms the backbone for daily operations. Management uses the MIS to gather data and, help with decision-making.

> **Flashback to N5**: In Module 1 of *Succeed with Personnel Management N5* you learned about the difference between data and information. Refer back to your notes on this before continuing.

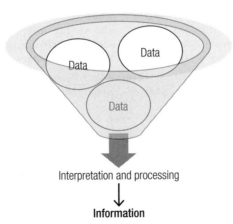

Interpretation and processing

↓

Information

Figure 5.2 Information is created from raw data.

DEFINITIONS

data – the facts, figures and detail we collect. It is bits of information, not the information itself. These bits of information are in a raw, unorganised context and rarely meaningful on its own.

information – the interpretation, processing and organising of the collected data to make these facts, figures and detail into something useful and in context

Management Information System (MIS) – the application of information technology to provide management with much-needed information to organise, evaluate and efficiently manage different departments and the organisation as a whole

---

5.1.1 Aims and objectives

The **HRIS** is a component of the Management Information System (MIS). The HRIS, also known as a Human Resource Information System, focuses on and manages Human Resource related issues and departments. The HR software allows all HR related activities and processes to occur electronically. Some of the purposes of using an HRIS include:

- using software or online solutions to enter data, track and save data for the Human Resource Management (HRM) to use
- providing valuable information for the recruitment process and payroll management
- storing and processing every single employee's data such as their names, addresses, identity numbers, work permit information (if applicable), payroll, attendance record, work performance, benefits, and information about their dependent(s)
- simplifying the management of the day-to-day HR processes and activities.

Did you know? The terms 'aims' and 'objectives' are often used **interchangeably** when referring to organisational goals. However, aims generally refer to the overall purpose or reason for doing something, while objectives tend to be more specific targets that an organisation would like to achieve.

Example 5.1

In Starting point, you saw how Nissan introduced HRIS with the aim of transforming human resources throughout the entire company and reducing costs across the globe. Nissan planned to achieve these aims by meeting their specific objectives of having standardised employee information and HR practices worldwide.

Allows all HR related activities and processes to occur electronically.	HRIS use software or online solutions to enter data, track and save data.
The HRIS is very valuable for the recruitment process and payroll management.	The HRM can store and process every single employee's data.

Figure 5.3 The aims of the HRIS

DEFINITIONS

HRIS – joining of the key human resource activities and functions with information technology (IT) through HR software

interchangeable – to put each of two things or people in the other's place; that can be exchanged without any effect

Power break 5.1   INDIVIDUAL WORK

Read the following scenario carefully and then answer the questions that follow.

Thuli has recently been hired as the HR Manager at a large clothing manufacturer with over 500 employees. Although the previous manager kept detailed and accurate employee records, everything had always been processed manually and stored as hard copies in a filing room. The HR clerks often forgot to put a file back or misplaced it and filed it under the incorrect department. This system made it very difficult for Thuli to access information quickly or meet deadlines when preparing reports for management meetings.

1   Explain the difference between data and information with the aid of relevant examples.
2   List some of the basic human resources tasks that could be computerised.
3   Do you think this organisation should implement an HRIS system? Give reasons for your answer.

5.1.2 Advantages of computerised information systems in practice

As we mentioned in the starting point of this module, organisations operate in a very complex and **dynamic environment**. The HRIS system helps the organisation to improve the traditional HR processes within this ever-changing environment. In Table 5.1 is a summary of some of the advantages of a computerised information system.

Table 5.1 Advantages of computerised information systems (HRIS)

Advantage	Explanation
Speed	Computerised information systems are extremely fast. Gaining access to an employee's information is quick and easy, by just pressing a button. Timeous information will enhance effective decision-making by management.
Accuracy	Computerised information systems are very accurate. The key to this accurate information is the computer operator correctly capturing the data or other instructions from management. The system would never make a mistake.
Costs	A computerised information system reduces the use of paper. The organisation saves paper costs by not using paper for reports, forms and files.
Strategic planning	The computerised information system can link with other systems to provide more information to make better and more calculated decisions.
Sharing of information	Organisations can use a network to share information. Sharing information improves the organisation's communication and ability to make more informed decisions.

DEFINITION

dynamic environment – an environment that is always changing and making progress

Table 5.1 Advantages of computerised information systems (HRIS) (*Cont.*)

Advantage	Explanation
Controlled access	Computerised information systems restrict any unauthorized access to the system, which protect the privacy and confidentiality of the information. You need a password to gain access.
Healthier working conditions	As mentioned above, the organisation saves on paper costs by using a computerised information system. Organisations these days are under pressure to "go green", being environmentally friendly, and by using less paper the organisation will be able to do just that.
Long-term cost benefits	The initial capital expense to set-up the HRIS might be high, but the long-term benefits and cost savings, far outweigh these costs.
Effective staff	The computerised information system will help management to manage the staff much better. Information about an employee's qualifications, experience and skills, is easy to access. Management can then utilise staff skills in the best way and thus ensure staff productivity.

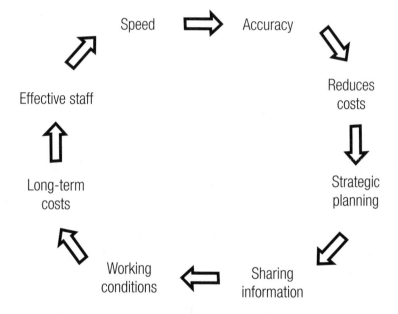

Figure 5.4 Advantages of a computerised information system

The HRIS issue

Previous to Diamond Solutions, DIACO Inc. had been using 2 different in-house applications to process their payroll. Senior Programmer/ System Analyst Rene Meyer explains DIACO's dissatisfaction with these systems: "We cannot remember one time in the past ten years that we had a problem-free payroll run. Many times, it would take weeks to work out the problems of one week's payroll." Employees' deductions and accruals often times had to be re-calculated manually, wasting many hours of DIACO's time. They needed an HRIS software solution that could streamline their payroll process, give them broader functionality, and automatically process multiple payrolls every month under different employee pay structures. The need for a more efficient and productive process payroll lead DIACO to search for an alternative in-house solution.

Read the article above and then answer the questions that follow.

1 What was the problem with their initial in-house solutions?
2 DIACO Inc.'s needs for a new HRIS can also be seen as advantages of this new system. List these advantages.

5.1.3 Design, development, implementation and evaluation of an effective human resource management system

Creating an effective human resource management system is not an easy task. A system that is poorly designed or was implemented in too much of a hurry may cause even more problems than having no computerised system at all! For example, delays in processing the organisation's payroll may lead to lower productivity levels or strikes by disgruntled employees; HR staff can become demotivated from working overtime to re-calculate incorrect wages and salaries; managers may make poor decisions due to a lack of accurate and timely information.

Organisations need to follow appropriate procedures to ensure that each task of setting up the human resource management system is carried out correctly. Figure 5.5 illustrates these tasks.

Figure 5.5 The procedures for creating an effective human resources system

Let's take a look at each of these tasks in more detail.

Designing an effective human resource management system

HRIS systems are usually designed in a modular manner to make them more flexible to the needs of each specific organisation. This means that smaller organisations can purchase a basic system and then add on additional modules as their workforce grows and their HR needs expand and change.

The core database or master file is where all employee information is captured and maintaine, for example employee names, identity numbers, addresses, date of employment, qualifications, skills, emergency contact details, etc. All other additional modules, such as payroll processing and performance management, must access this core database to draw on information. When information in the core module is updated, these changes are immediately reflected in all the other modules. This design ensures the accuracy and consistency of employee data across the entire HRIS system. The actual design of the HRIS software can only start after the system requirements have been finalised, which takes places during the development steps.

Developing an effective human resource management system

The steps in Table 5.2 can be used to identify or create the human resource management system which will best fit the organisation's particular needs.

Table 5.2 Steps in creating the human resource management system

Step	Explanation
Step 1	**Identify objectives** Identify the human resources need for the system and any problems that need to be addressed. Consider human resource issues, including recruiting, hiring, training, managing and terminating employees.
Step 2	**Feasibility study** Consider all the available systems that would satisfy the needs of the organisation.
Step 3	**System analysis** Analyse the system you identified. Determine if the system will serve the purpose it is required to do.
Step 4	**System design** A model system is now being designed to address all the objectives you set.
Step 5	**Programme specification** Select the best possible and ideal system. The hardware and software have been set up. Test the programme specifications to see if it accurately addresses the needs of the organisation.
Step 6	**System Implementation** Implement the system into the organisation. Develop training programmes and provide detailed written documentation for the users of the system.
Step 7	**System evaluation** The system must be carefully monitored to make sure it delivers what it is intended and required to do. Identify any barriers that are preventing the success of the system in the organisation.

Implementing an effective human resource management system

Implementation refers to the process of putting something into practice. Once the best system has been identified or developed (step 5), it then needs to be put into operation in the organisation (step 6).

Providing adequate and appropriate training is an important part of the implementation phase. Initially, the HR managers and employees will need extensive training from the system developers. At a later stage, the HR staff can train managers from other departments in how to submit information to the system or request information from it. Having a fancy computerised system is of no value if nobody understands how to use it properly.

Did you know? A study done by SilverRoad solutions showed the following:

- Up to 90% of organisations are unhappy with their HR systems.
- The one area that receives inadequate attention is the actual implementation process.
- Many problems with the system might have been avoided if the implementation team had addressed the issue adequately.

Evaluating an effective human resource management system

Evaluation (step 7) forms part of the control process. The chosen system must be monitored to determine whether it is achieving the desired outcomes or objectives that were identified in step 1. Employees and managers who use the system regularly are a valuable source of feedback and can usually make recommendations on improvements. An ideal system should be adding value to the organisation and making the HR functions more comfortable to perform.

We will take a closer look at some of the criteria which can be used to evaluate the system in the next section.

Software packages with prepacked personnel systems

Most organisations cannot afford to pay developers to create their own HRIS software from scratch. However, a wide range of existing software packages with prepacked personnel systems is readily available for use in practice. Most of these software packages are modular in design, and some can even be customised to a certain extent. Human resources software may include many prepacked modules such as:

- recruitment
- employee management
- skills development
- vehicle management
- performance management
- leave administration
- occupational health and safety
- employment equity.

Example 5.2

You can learn more about some of the software resources that are available in South Africa by visiting the following websites:

- SmartHR (www.smarthr.co.za)
- Roubler (www.roubler.com/za)
- Peopleplus (www.peopleplus.co.za)
- Sage VIP / Sage Pastel (www.sage.com/za)
- HR Manage (www.peopleres.co.za)
- CRS Technologies (www.crs.co.za)
- Accsys (www.accsys.co.za)

There are also many other human resources software packages which are available both locally and internationally. This can make it rather difficult for organisations to choose the best software provider. The criteria in Table 5.3 can be used to evaluate the various software packages before purchasing them.

Table 5.3 Criteria to evaluate various software packages

Criteria	Explanation
User-friendly	Not only professionals should be able to use the system. The HRIS should be easy to use; user-friendly, for everyone that may be using the system. Before the organisation commits to a new system, they should ask for a trial. That way the organisation can determine if it is, in fact, user-friendly and avoid frustrating the users.
Costs	The costs of a new system are always a factor management needs to evaluate. The HRIS that you choose should be within the current budget. It is also important to consider future costs like updates, subscription fees and training.
User and data security	The information captured on an HRIS is typically confidential. The system must secure employees and other related parties' information. The system must be secure and only allow authorised personnel to gain access. The system must also be secure against outside threats and viruses.
Support	The vendor should provide training and general support for the users. Some of the vendors provide you with a support line to call for assistance or online support services where the users can type in their queries. Swift feedback and support are very important for the HRIS to be successful.
Maintenance	The maintenance and updates should be smooth and affordable for the HR department. The system must also meet the dynamic demands of the organisation.

Did you know? In 1983 a training management system called Educos was started in South Africa. This software has since grown into a fully integrated HCM and Payroll system that has expanded throughout Africa and internationally. You can learn more at http://www.educos.co.za

5.1.4 Applications of HRIS

The HRIS is only beneficial to the organisation if it serves the various HR functions that it is supposed to. Figure 5.6 illustrates the various HR functions where HRIS can be applied to improve the management of organisational and employee information.

Figure 5.6 The applications of HRIS

Performance management

In the long term, the system will be able to record and track an employee from one position to the next position. In the short term, the system will capture, analyse and interpret performance appraisal ratings. This is important for management to take action in improving poor performances, and also, to reward excellent performances.

Salary administration

The HRIS system is useful for capturing data such as names, titles, addresses and salaries of employees. It is also useful for keeping a record of salary and position history, reporting structures, performance appraisal history and important private employee information.

The administration of disciplinary records is especially critical for an organisation. Who is suspended? Who is demoted? Who is dismissed? Dates and times of the offence, the type of offence and the action taken against the employee can be recorded accurately. The accuracy is important for the fairness and validity of the disciplinary action.

Health and safety

The HRIS can keep record of any injuries and/or accidents in the organisation. Health and safety are of the utmost importance. The HR department will use the system to record and track employees' sick leave, injuries, accidents and hospitalisations. Specific employee health and safety information, like diabetes or epilepsy, is easy to access. The HR department uses this information to plan training sessions and to avoid future injuries and accidents.

Education and training

It is important for the organisation to keep track of education and training records and is linked to the performance appraisal records. This information is useful in the development of employees, which is key to the prosperous future for the organisation. The HR department can determine where there is a specific need or just training and development, in general, to keep up with the latest trends and technology.

The HR department can identify a need for education, training and development or the employee can book or request on the HRIS, via a self-service function.

Payroll

As mentioned before, all payroll related information is captured on the HRIS. Salaries are reviewed and adjusted every year, in line with performance appraisals. Any changes to each employee can then easily be integrated with the financial department's system. This is important because the organisation is guided by budgets.

Employment/Recruitment

As soon as an employee resigns, retires or the organisation expands, the HRIS will alarm the HR department of the future employment needs of the organisation. The HR department can then be pro-active in starting the recruitment process early. This will give them the best opportunity to find the best candidate to fill the vacant position.

The system will give the HR department information about current personnel that will be able to fill the position and meet the required criteria, but also point out areas or positions that will require external recruitment.

Benefits administration

The HR department uses the HRIS system to determine which employees qualify for fringe benefits. The system makes the administration of benefits easy and quick to access. Benefits administration is linked to the payroll function.

Power break 5.4 GROUP WORK

1 Draw a mind map that illustrates the various applications of HRIS in the human resources function.
2 Add examples of the organisational and employee information which would form part of each of the applications which you identified in question 1.

UNIT 5.2 Spreadsheets and graphic representations

5.2.1 Use of spreadsheets to provide information for management

A spreadsheet is a worksheet that has numbered rows and columns in a tabular format. Spreadsheets provide an orderly way to analyse and present data. They are especially useful for organising large amounts of financial or numerical data. Computerised spreadsheets also allow for data to be manipulated through mathematical formulas and then presented as charts or graphs. Microsoft Excel is one of the most popular software programmes for spreadsheets.

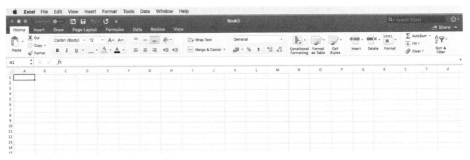

Figure 5.7 Spreadsheets in Microsoft Excel

When to use a spreadsheet

Spreadsheets can be used for various purposes in the organisation. Some of the most common uses include:

- managing accounts and maintaining customer records
- managing projects and programs
- strategic analysis and informing business decisions
- office administration and record keeping
- inventory tracking and supplier management
- recording and storing employee information.

Figure 5.8 A spreadsheet showing budgeted figures

> **Did you know?** Spreadsheets were once a popular alternative to HRIS, especially in small organisations with fewer employees and simple HR processes. However, most organisations have realised that specific HR software provides a more integrated and accurate solution for capturing, storing, analysing and presenting HR information.

Power break 5.5 INDIVIDUAL WORK

Use the spreadsheet below to answer the questions that follow.

	A	B	C	D	E	F	G	H
1	Employee nu	Date of birth	Title	Surname	Initials	Department	Position	Start date
2	1	12/04/1977	Mr	Majola	T	Finance	Accountant	22/05/2007
3	2	31/10/1996	Ms	Sewnath	P	HR	Clerk	26/11/2010
4	3	23/04/1965	Ms	Sibiya	L	Sales	Manager	13/02/2012
5	4	02/12/1975	Mrs	Swart	M	Production	Foreman	30/10/2018

1 Who is the youngest employee in this organisation?
2 Which employees have birthdays in April?
3 In which column would you find information about employees' job titles?
4 How many female employees does this organisation have?

5.2.2 Use of graphic representations to provide information for management

People understand information better when they can see it visually. Graphs and charts are graphic representations of data. With graphs and charts, you can see comparisons, trends and regressions. Microsoft Excel is one programme you can use to create data charts.

Figure 5.9 The chart tool in Microsoft Excel

Different types of graphs

Line graphs

A line graph is a graphical device that displays information as a series of data connected by straight line segments. This is the most basic and versatile chart and is the most frequently used form of a chart. You can use a line graph when working with percentages or raw data numbers of whatever you measure, for example, the number of people, the temperature in degrees or the height in metres.

The line graph works on a horizontal and vertical axis. The horizontal axis (x-axis, left to right) usually shows time. The vertical axis (y-axis, upright) shows variable data, for example, numbers or percentages. The line joins points on the graph where the x-axis and y-axis meet, showing how the variable increased or decreased over time.

When to use a line graph

Line graphs are used to track changes over periods. When smaller changes exist, line graphs are better to use than bar graphs because it is easier to see a small change on a line graph.

Line graphs can also be used to compare changes over the same period for more than one group. For example, the human resources department can use the averages of the staff turnover over the last five years and plot that on a line graph. When the human resource manager discusses staff turnover with the board of directors, they can visually see if there is an increase (going up) or a decrease (going down) in the number of people leaving the organisation and the number of people being appointed every year.

This will give the board of directors a visual on the trends (the dotted line) over the last few years as well. Positive trends show that staff turnover decreased over time; negative trends show that staff turnover increased.

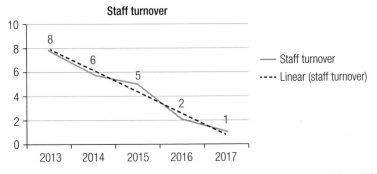

Figure 5.10 A line graph showing a positive trend in staff turnover between 2013 and 2017

Power break 5.6 INDIVIDUAL WORK

Use the line graph showing the percentage of cars purchased by fuel type (gasoline or diesel) between 1985 and 2008 (below) to answer the questions that follow.

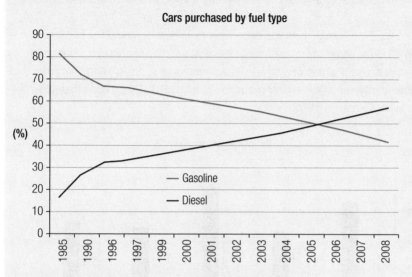

Cars purchased by fuel type

1 In which year were the most diesel cars purchased?
2 In which year were the least diesel cars purchased?
3 In which year were the same number of diesel and gasoline cars purchased?
4 What is the general trend?

Bar graphs

A bar graph (also called a bar chart) is a chart that uses either horizontal or vertical bars to show you how different categories of data compare. There are different types of bar charts: vertical bar graphs and horizontal bar graphs.

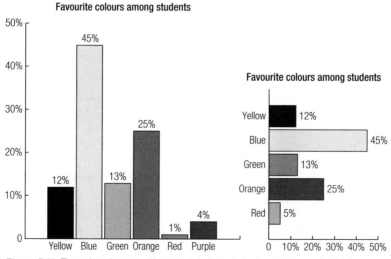

Figure 5.11 Examples of a vertical bar graph (left) and a horizontal bar graph (right)

When to use a bar graph

Bar graphs are used to compare things between different groups or to track changes over time. However, when trying to measure changes over time, bar graphs are best when the changes are larger. Use a line graph for smaller changes as they are difficult to see on a bar graph.

For example, if the human resource department wants to compare the number of men versus women in the organisation over the last five years, they should use a bar graph. They may want to use the ratio of men versus woman for their equity report, which would show a figure for men and women, for example, 15:19 in 2017. That means there are 19 women for every 15 men in the company.

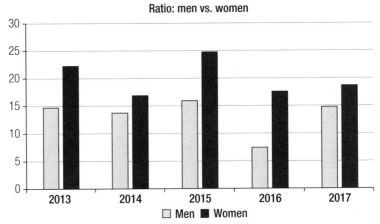

Figure 5.12 A vertical bar graph showing the number of men and women in an organisation between 2013 and 2017

Power break 5.7   INDIVIDUAL WORK

Use the bar graph below to answer the questions that follow.

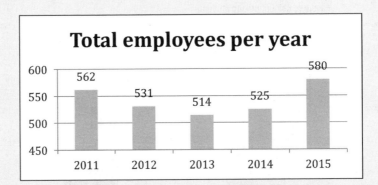

1 In which year was this organisation's workforce the largest?
2 How many new employees joined the organisation between 2013 and 2014?
3 Did employee numbers increase or decrease between 2012 and 2013?
4 How many employees did this organisation have in 2011?

Pie charts

A pie chart is a circular graphic that shows percentages or proportional data. The circle is divided into slices to illustrate the proportions, just like how you might cut up a pie. All the percentages in a pie chart must add up to 100%.

The pie chart in Figure 5.13 shows the results of a survey to see which colour students like best. You can see that the biggest slice of the pie is for the colour blue. This means that the highest percentage of students like the colour blue (45%). This means blue is the most popular colour. Orange is the second most popular; green is the third most popular; yellow is the fourth most popular colour, and red is the least popular colour.

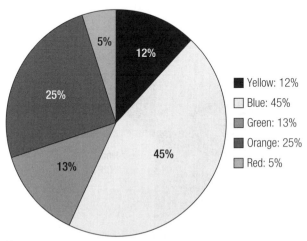

Figure 5.13 A pie chart showing students' favourite colours

You survey with your friends to find the kind of movie they like best:

Favourite type of movie				
Comedy	**Action**	**Romance**	**Drama**	**SciFi**
4	6	6	1	4

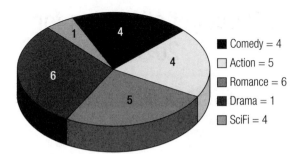

Figure 15.14 A pie chart showing the favourite type of movie

It is easy to see which movie is most liked, and which one is the least popular.

* Most popular = Romance (30%)
* Least popular = Drama (5%)

To calculate the percentage:

- There were 20 participants in total.
- 4 of the 20 like comedy the most.
- 4 ÷ 20 × 100 = 20%
- The total of all the percentages will always be 100%.

When to use a pie chart

Pie charts are best to use when you are trying to compare parts of a whole. Pie charts are not useful for showing changes over time. The human resources manager of a firm might use a pie chart to show the percentages of the labour cost for each department in the organisation. As you can see in the pie chart below, in this particular organisation the largest percentage goes to Finance (36%).

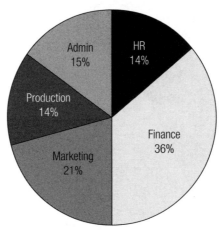

Figure 5.15 A pie chart showing the division of the labour budget by department

Power break 5.8 INDIVIDUAL WORK

Use the pie chart below to answer the questions that follow.

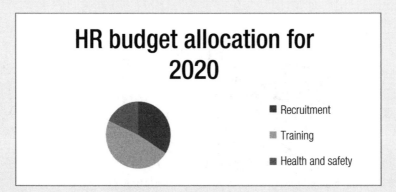

1 Which expense forms the largest part of the HR budget for 2020?
3 To which HR function is the smallest percentage of the budget allocated?
3 What are the benefits of using a pie chart to illustrate information?

What have we learned about Personnel Management and where to next?

In this module, we learned about information systems and graphic representations for managing human resources. We started by discussing the aims and objectives of human resources information (data) systems (HRIS) in the work environment and the advantages of computerised information systems in practice. We went on to briefly describe the procedures (task list) for the design, development (steps) and the implementation and evaluation of effective human resource management systems. Then we looked at software packages with prepacked personnel systems to be used in practice and criteria to evaluate them. We also discussed the content of organisational and employee information. Lastly, we looked at the use of spreadsheets, graphs and graphics presentations to provide information for management.

Revisiting the learning objectives

Now that you have completed this module, let's see if you have achieved the learning outcomes that were set out at the beginning of the module. In the table below, we summarise what you have learned for each objective.

Learning objective	What have you learned	✓
Discuss the aims and objectives of human resources information (data) systems (HRIS) in the work environment.	• Allows all HR related activities and processes to occur electronically. • HRIS use software or online solutions to enter data, track and save data. • The HRIS is very valuable for the recruitment process and payroll management. • The HRM can store and process every single employee's data.	☐
Explain the advantages of computerised information systems in practice.	Advantages of computerised information systems in practice: • Speed • Accuracy • Costs • Strategic planning • Sharing of information • Controlled access • Healthier working conditions • Long-term cost benefits • Effective staff	☐

Describe the procedures (task list) for the design, development (steps) and the implementation and evaluation of effective human resource management systems briefly.	The steps in the development of effective human resource management systems: Step 1: Identify human resources need Step 2: Consider all the available systems Step 3: Analyse the system you identified. Step 4: A model system is now being designed. Step 5: Select the best possible and ideal system. Step 6: Implement the system into the organisation. Step 7: The system must be closely monitored. ☐
List software packages with prepacked personnel systems to be used in practice and criteria to evaluate them.	Various software packages are available as per example. ☐ Criteria for evaluating software packages include: • user-friendly • costs • user and data security • support • maintenance ☐
Describe the content of the two major classes of information, namely organisational and employee information.	HRIS can be applied to the management of information in the following HR functions: • Performance appraisal • Salary administration • Health and safety • Education and training • Payroll • Employment/recruitment • Benefits administration ☐
Demonstrate the use of spreadsheets and graphs to provide information for management.	Understand and know when and how to use spreadsheets and graphs to provide information. ☐
Demonstrate the use of graphic presentations to provide information for management.	Understand and know when to use each of the following types of graphic representations: • Line graphs • Bar graphs • Pie charts. ☐

Assessment

1. True or false questions

Indicate whether the following statements are TRUE or FALSE. Write only 'true' or 'false' next to the question number.

1.1 The HRIS disperses information throughout the organisation.

1.2 The computerised HRIS help with current skills inventories of staff and with human resources planning.

1.3 The HRIS use software or online solutions to enter data, to share data with others and to save data.

1.4 Controlled access restrict any unauthorised access to the HRIS.

1.5 Payroll is the employee who leaves the organisation.

(5 x 2)

[10]

2. Multiple-choice questions

Choose the correct answer from the various options provided. Write only A, B, C, D, E or F next to the question number.

Column A		Column B	
2.1	The system must be user-friendly.	A	MIS
2.2	Gather, complete and analyse information	B	HRIS
2.3	facts, figures and detail we collect.	C	data
2.4	interpretation, processing and organising of the collected information.	D	information
2.5	The system must be closely monitored.	E	criteria for evaluating a computerised HRIS.
		F	Last step of the implementation and evaluation of the HRIS.

(5 x 2)

[10]

3. Short questions

Briefly answer the following questions:

3.1 Define the following:

    3.1.1 Management Information System (MIS) (4)

    3.1.2 Human Resource Information System (HRIS) (4)

3.2 Name any THREE areas where the computerised HRIS can be implemented to help management making a success of their business. (3 x 2)

3.3 Explain to staff the objectives/aims of an HRIS. (3 x 2)

[20]

4. Long questions

Answer the following questions as comprehensively as you can:

4.1 Discuss the advantages of a computerised HRIS. (9 x 2)

4.2 It is important that management should make the right decision when deciding on a computerised HRIS.

Explain the criteria helping management to make the right decision. (5 x 2)

4.3 Discuss the steps in the design and development of an HRIS. (7 x 2)

4.4 What is the difference between data and information? (2 x 2)

4.5 Name and discuss the important functions (application) of the HRIS in detail. (6 x 4)

[70]

Total: [110]

REFERENCES

'Adams' equity theory'. Available at https://www.mindtools.com/pages/article/newLDR_96.htm [Accessed on 11 July 2018].

'Women are one of the fastest growing groups of car consumers'. Available at https://www.wheels24.co.za/News/Guides_and_Lists/women-are-one-of-the-fastest-growing-groups-of-car-consumers-study-20180811

Brits, S & Coetzee, Z. 2016. Succeed in Personnel Management N4. Cape Town: Oxford University Press.

Dworzanowski-Venter, B. 2015. Succeed in Labour Relations N6. Cape Town: Oxford University Press.

Formal communication network. Available at https://businessjargons.com/formal-communication-network.html [Accessed on 17 August 2018].

French, J. (2012, September 26). Communication in the Digital Age. Available at www.entrepreneurmag.co.za. [Accessed on 6 August 2018].

Graham, M & Iyer, S. 2016. Succeed in Public Relations N5. Cape Town: Oxford University Press.

Graham, M & Iyer, S. 2017. Succeed in Business and Entrepreneurship N5. Cape Town: Oxford University Press.

Hauptfleish, H & Rheeder, L. 2017. Succeed in Management Communication N4. Cape Town: Oxford University Press.

Herzberg, F. 1987. 'One more time: How do you motivate employees?' Harvard Business Review, September–October 1987.

International Journal of Teaching and Case Studies 4(2):95 - 11.4. HRIS at Nissan: a new era in human resource management. January 2013 Available at https://www.researchgate.net/publication/264820251_HRIS_at_Nissan_a_new_era_in_human_resource_management

Kreitner & Kinicki. Organizational Behaviour. McGraw-Hill.

Kroon, J (Ed). General Management, 'The Griffiths Commission'. Cape Town: Reprinted by permission of Pearson Business.

Maslow, Abraham H.; Frager, Robert D.; Fadiman, James, Motivation and personality, 3rd Edition, ©1987.

Mohammed, F, Abdullah, W. Human Resources Management: A Comprehensive Guide. Reprinted by permission of Pearson Business. 2002.

Mulder, PAGE 2010. Management by objectives (MBO). Available at https://www.toolshero.com/management/management-by-objectives-drucker/ [Accessed on 13 July 2018].

Nair, K & Ristić, D. 2013. Personnel Management N6. Troupant Publishers [Pty] Ltd.

Nel et al. Human Resources Management. 2008. 7th Edition. Cape Town: Oxford University Press.

Northouse, PAGE Trait Approach, SAGE Publishers. Available at https://www.sagepub.com/sites/default/files/upm-binaries/30933_Northouse_Chapter_2.pdf

Oxford Advanced Learner's Dictionary of Current English. 2015. 9th Edition. Oxford University Press.

Sincero, SM. 2012. 'Process of motivation'. Available at https://explorable.com/process-of-motivation [Accessed on 5 July 2018].

Situational Leadership® and Performance Readiness® are registered trademarks of Leadership Studies, Inc. Copyright © 1972-2017. All Rights Reserved.

Smit, R. 2016. Succeed in Sales Management N6. Cape Town: Oxford University Press.

The Leadership Grid® figure, Paternalism Figure and Opportunism from Leadership Dilemmas–Grid Solutions, by Robert R. Blake and Anne Adams McCanse (Formerly the Managerial Grid by Robert R. Blake and Jane S. Mouton). Houston: Gulf Publishing Company, (Grid Figure: PAGE 29, Paternalism Figure: page 30, Opportunism Figure: page 31). Copyright 1991 by Scientific Methods, Inc. Reproduced by permission of the owners.

Todd, N. 2017. 'Organisational expert Siphiwe Moyo's insights into keeping your employees motivated'. Available at www.entrepreneurmag.co.za [Accessed on 2 July 2018].

Van Staden, J. 2018. Succeed in Personnel Management N5. Cape Town: Oxford University Press.

Vroom, VH. 1964. Work and motivation. New York: John Wiley & Sons

Willson-Kirsten, H. Human Resources Management N6. Cape Town: Future Managers (Pty) Ltd.

ACKNOWLEDGEMENTS

Texts

page 11 Maslow, Abraham H.; Frager, Robert D.; Fadiman, James, Motivation and personality, 3rd Edition, ©1987; page 28 Todd, N. 2017. 'Organisational expert Siphiwe Moyo's insights into keeping your employees motivated'. Available at www.entrepreneurmag.co.za [Accessed on 2 July 2018]; page 36 French, J. (2012, September 26). *Communication in the Digital Age.* Available at www.entrepreneurmag.co.za. [Accessed on 6 August 2018]; page 72 'Women are one of the fastest growing groups of car consumers'. Available at https://www.wheels24.co.za/News/Guides_and_Lists/women-are-one-of-the-fastest-growing-groups-of-car-consumers-study-20180811; page 84 Kroon, J (Ed). General Management, 'The Griffiths Commission'. Cape Town: Reprinted by permission of Pearson Business; page 113 Kreitner & Kinicki. Organizational Behaviour. McGraw-Hill; page 119 The Leadership Grid® figure, Paternalism Figure and Opportunism from Leadership Dilemmas-Grid Solutions, by Robert R. Blake and Anne Adams McCanse (Formerly the Managerial Grid by Robert R. Blake and Jane S. Mouton). Houston: Gulf Publishing Company, (Grid Figure: PAGE 29, Paternalism Figure: page 30, Opportunism Figure: page 31). Copyright 1991 by Scientific Methods, Inc. Reproduced by permission of the owners; p; page 122-124 Situational Leadership® and Performance Readiness® are registered trademarks of Leadership Studies, Inc. Copyright © 1972-2017. All Rights Reserved.

Images

page 4 Shutterstock 273624035/Trueffelpix; page 5 Shutterstock 269821922 gpointstudio; page 7 Shutterstock 405959236 spectrumblue; page 17 Shutterstock 283640375 alekseiveprev; page 23 Shutterstock 38103676 nikkytok; page 24 Shutterstock 256521256 patpitchaya; page 27 Shutterstock 697232719 eclissi; page 36 Shutterstock 300374789 Rawpixel.com; page 37 Shutterstock 231559234 dizain; page 40 Shutterstock 1145812526 Indypendenz; page 40 Shutterstock 1048653074 fizkes; page 41 Shutterstock 246255295 JrCasas; page 43 Shutterstock 100344080 Andre Adams; page 45 Shutterstock 275751935 safriibrahim; page 49 Shutterstock 305380997 Victor Metelskiy; page 49 Shutterstock 453060997 Hsynff; page 49 cartoon; page 53 Shutterstock 346589825 Robert Kneschke; page 59 Shutterstock 551383783 Rawpixel.com; page 57 jmo0024 www.CartoonStock.com; page 59 Shutterstock 696697792 Bakhtiar Zein; page 60 mbcn3954 www.CartoonStock.com; page 63 Shutterstock 495535387; page 69 Shutterstock 696697792; page 70 Shutterstock 277482842 Rawpixel.com; page 72 Shutterstock 280182368 shuvector; page 73 Shutterstock 141199678 Vitchanan Photography; page 75 Shutterstock 447950908 wavebreakmedia; page 79 Shutterstock 522965386 Jacob Lund; page 82 Shutterstock 275800256 Monkey Business Images; page 87 Shutterstock 725984596 Akira Kaelyn; page 87 Shutterstock 650561296 Melissa Hani; page 87 Shutterstock 574590628 garagestock; page 87 Shutterstock 582569893 fizkes; page 87 Shutterstock 1034490523 Scarlette; page 90 Shutterstock 218755333; Rawpixel.com; page 92 Shutterstock 239157490 Digital Storm; page 95 Shutterstock 1022439892 fizkes; page 100 Shutterstock 226243561 sirtravelalot; page 101 Pixabay 2009183 johnhain; page 102 Pixabay 1767672 johnhain; page 110 Getty Images Europe GYI0000631237; page 127 Pixabay 913043 Tumiso; page 128 Pixabay 1580143 geralt; page 128 Pixabay 985542 Merio; page 129 Shutterstock 687246 geralt; page 133 Shutterstock 642768262 pathdoc; page 134 Shutterstock 738111628 EtiAmmos.

GLOSSARY

achievement a thing that somebody has done successfully, using their own effort

additive all group members perform the same task to improve the bigger task

affiliation a person's connection with a group or organisation

align to be in the correct position in relation to something else

allegations accusing somebody of doing something that is wrong or illegal

ambiguous having more than one meaning

approach a way of going towards something, to take preliminary steps towards an accomplishment

asset a person or thing that is valuable or useful

attitude the way that you think or feel about something

autonomy the ability to act and make decisions without being controlled by anyone

cohesion a process of sticking together and forming a united whole while following the group's goals and objectives

complexity being formed of many parts; difficult to understand

conformity the behaviour or actions that follow the accepted rules of the workplace

confrontational to be in a tense or unpleasant situation that you must face

conjunctive every group member has a different task to do fo`r the group to complete a task

data the facts, figures and detail we collect. It is bits of information, not the information itself. These bits of information are in a raw, unorganised context and rarely meaningful on its own.

decision-making the process of making choices by identifying a decision, gathering information, and assessing alternative solutions

decodes finds the meaning of something

deferential to be respectful towards something or somebody

demotivated when somebody feels that it is not worth making an effort

desire a strong wish to have or do something

disgruntled annoyed or disappointed

disjunctive a group task is completed when a single solution or decision of an individual is adopted by the group distort to twist or change facts so that they are no longer correct or true

distorted to change the shape or sound of something so that it is no longer clear

diverse very different from each other, for example, different literacy levels, backgrounds, cultures, language differences, etc.

dynamic environment an environment that is always changing and making progress

efficiently doing something well with no waste of time or money

encodes changes thoughts or ideas into language, letters, symbols, etc.

entitles gives somebody the right to have or do something

equity a situation in which everyone is treated equally

ethics moral principles that control or influence a person's behaviour

expectancy the state of expecting or hoping that something will happen

favouritism the act of unfairly treating one person better than others because you like them better

formal group a group deliberately developed by managers to achieve organisational goals

frontline employees employees who deal directly with customers or the public

grapevine the circulation of rumours and unofficial information

group two or more individuals interacting with each other to achieve a particular goal or meet specific needs

hierarchical when people are organised from the most to least powerful

hierarchy a system that ideas or beliefs can be arranged into

HRIS joining of the key human resource activities and functions with information technology (IT) through HR software

imbalance a situation in which things are not in balance, which causes problems

implement to make something start to happen

incentive something that encourages you to do something

informal group a group formed by employees of an organisation to achieve their own goals or to meet their own needs

information the interpretation, processing and organising of the collected data to make these facts, figures and detail into something useful and in context

intentional done deliberately

interchangeable to put each of two things or people in the other's place; that can be exchanged without any effect

intercultural existing or happening between different cultures

interdependent two or more people or groups that depend on each other

interpersonal communication connected with relationships between people

jargon words or expressions used by a certain profession or group

leadership the ability to influence a group of people towards setting and achieving a goal

management the ability to coordinate and organise a group of people and their activities towards achievement of the outlined goals

Management Information System (MIS) the application of information technology to provide management with much-needed information to organise, evaluate and efficiently manage different departments and the organisation as a whole

managerial leadership a leadership style where a leader can reshuffle his or her roles and responsibilities according to the situation to accomplish goals.

manipulation a technique of influencing or forcing someone to do what you want

mental stimulus something that is more interesting and challenging to your mind

misconceptions beliefs or ideas that are not based on correct information

monopolisation a way of controlling or owning something; having complete control

monotony boring, lack of variety

morale the amount of confidence or enthusiasm, etc., that a person or a group has at a particular time

overstep to go beyond what is normal or allowed

participative allowing everyone to give opinions and to help make decisions

perceptions ideas or beliefs that you have as the result of how you see something

power the ability to control people or things

productivity the rate at which a worker, a company or a country produces goods

rank to give something a particular position on a scale according to importance

ratio the relationship between two groups of people or things

resources a supply of something that is available for use, such as money

slang informal language used and understood by a specific social group

strategies methods to achieve a particular purpose, or solve a problem

subordinates persons who have a position with less authority and power

theory an explanation for why certain things work and how things materialise; based on an idea that one can test, and not on speculation or a guess

timeously in good time; early enough

trait a particular quality in your personality

vocabulary all the words that a person knows or uses

INDEX